# anti-inflammatory
# COOKBOOK

Publications International, Ltd.

**Pictured on the back cover** *(clockwise from top right):* Quinoa & Mango Salad *(page 142),* Roasted Salmon with New Potatoes and Red Onions *(page 60),* Cranberry Fruit Salad *(page 158),* Cabbage Patch Juice *(page 163),* Cantaloupe Strawberry Sunrise *(page 174),* and Zucchini and Sweet Potato Stuffed Peppers *(page 106).*

**Contributing Writer:** Jacqueline B Marcus, MS, RDN, LDN, CNS, FADA, FAND

ISBN: 978-1-64030-335-5

Manufactured in China.

8 7 6 5 4 3 2 1

**Microwave Cooking:** Microwave ovens vary in wattage. Use the cooking times as guidelines and check for doneness before adding more time.

# table of
# CONTENTS

understanding inflammation...4

small bites......................24

soups & stews ...................38

main-dish salads & entrées ...58

meatless meals ..................92

sides & salads .................114

desserts & snacks .............146

sippers & juices ...............160

index.........................188

# understanding
# INFLAMMATION

## what is inflammation?

A painful cut that puffs and reddens. A skinned knee that is sore to the touch. A reddened eye that itches and tears. These conditions may signify *acute inflammation*, a complex biological response to what the body perceives as potentially harmful injury or stimuli.

Unending stomach or intestinal cramps and discomfort. Constant joint and muscular aches and pains. Lingering sinusitis and allergic-type symptoms. These conditions may signal *chronic inflammation*, a complex biological response to longer-term "wear and tear" on the body with multiple causes and outcomes.

### ACUTE INFLAMMATION

Acute inflammation is the early and sometimes immediate response by the human body to potentially harmful bacteria or an injury to bodily tissues. In acute inflammation, damaged cells, foreign invaders such as bacteria and viruses, irritants, and pathogens, bombard the body and activate blood vessels, immune cells, and molecular modulators to respond and repair.

The onset of acute inflammation may last just a few days and it generally improves on its own. If acute inflammation lasts longer and if the inflamed site becomes abscessed, then this may mark infection or a longer, more chronic condition.

Acute appendicitis, bronchitis, infected ingrown nails, infective meningitis, physical trauma, sinusitis, skin abrasions, sore throat from cold or flu, or tonsillitis may trigger acute inflammation.

### CHRONIC INFLAMMATION

Chronic inflammation is typically longer in duration than acute inflammation and due more to "use and abuse" than acute injuries.

Chronic inflammation may be initiated by pathogens that the body has a difficult time destroying. It may not be as noticeable as acute inflammation—especially if sensory nerve endings are not close enough to affected areas to register pain. The onset may be slow, starting from days and lasting from months to years. Symptoms of chronic inflammation may include abdominal, chest, joint and muscular pain; fatigue; fever; mouth sores; and rashes.

Factors that contribute to chronic inflammation may include alcohol ingestion, diet, drug use, environmental conditions, genes, inactivity, oral health, smoking, stress, weight, and *autoimmune diseases*.

*Autoimmune diseases* are illnesses that occur when body tissues are attacked by the immune system. For example, lupus and rheumatoid arthritis may have inflammatory origins as well as pernicious anemia and Type 1 diabetes.

Conditions and diseases that may be caused by chronic inflammation may include active hepatitis, arthritis (gouty, osteo-, psoriatic, and rheumatoid), asthma, Crohn's disease, chronic peptic ulcer, diverticula disease, fibromyalgia, periodontitis, sinusitis, tuberculosis, ulcerative colitis, and more.

Chronic inflammation may lead to thickening and scaring of connective tissues and even tissue death. Longer term, untreated chronic inflammation may cause more complicated health problems, such as atherosclerosis, bone disease, diabetes, hypertension, and some cancers.

## IMMUNE HEALTH

Since inflammation has both acute and chronic expressions, it is difficult to pinpoint their relationship to immune health. Some generic factors may also come into play.

People with healthy immune systems are generally able to defend themselves against some shorter and longer-term inflammatory conditions or diseases. They may have acquired "adaptive" immunity that developed after an infection or vaccination, inherited a healthy immune system, taken excellent care of their health, been lucky, or benefitted by many of these factors.

# identification, treatment, and control

## IDENTIFICATION

Acute inflammatory disease may be identified by an abrasion, contusion, redness, or swelling. Chronic inflammation may be more complicated to identify; therefore blood tests, medical histories, physical exams, X-rays, or other electronic procedures may be necessary.

For example, *C-reactive protein (CRP)* is a blood test marker for infection or inflammation. The liver produces C-reactive protein that rises in response to inflammation. A CRP level over 3.0 mg/dL may pose a higher-than-normal risk of certain chronic diseases such as cardiovascular disease.

## TREATMENT

Acute inflammation is typically treated with topical analgesics and other over-the-counter medications unless it persists and becomes infected. Then, medical attention is advised.

Controlling chronic inflammation often involves a combination of treatment approaches. These may include behavior modification, diet, exercise, medications, physical therapy, rest or sleep, yoga, or surgery in some cases. Efforts should be taken to avoid or modify activities that aggravate or induce the most pain.

Many drugs may help decrease joint pain, inflammation, overall discomfort and swelling—independently or in combination with others.

Cannabis, ginger, and turmeric are some of the herbal remedies that may also be used to treat various types of inflammation. The use of drugs and herbs to relieve inflammation should be under the guidance of health care professionals.

### CONTROL: DIET AND NUTRITION

One of the most important and often overlooked methods of prevention, treatment, and control of inflammation is diet and nutrition.

The building blocks of a nutritious diet: carbohydrates, fats, proteins, vitamins, and minerals that are found in a variety of lean proteins, lower-fat dairy products, fresh fruits and vegetables, healthy fats, nuts and seeds, and whole grains provide the foundation of anti-inflammatory eating.

Other substances such as chocolate, coffee and tea, fermented foods, herbs and spices, and pre- and probiotics, along with adequate hydration and supplements, if needed, round out a spectrum of anti-inflammatory measures.

Hard evidence for one type of anti-inflammatory method over another may be lacking, but collectively some of these approaches may be effective. It is best to check any dietary approaches with a health care provider.

## foods to use, limit, and avoid

An anti-inflammatory approach to diet and nutrition is mostly founded on a Mediterranean-type diet that emphasizes the following foods with fiber-rich carbohydrates, lean proteins, healthy fats, and disease-fighting vitamins and minerals:

- **Cold-water fish** (herring, mackerel, salmon, sardines, and tuna) with omega 3-fatty acids.

- **Fresh fruits and vegetables** (berries, oranges, broccoli, and cauliflower) with plant-based *phytonutrients* (*antioxidants, flavonoids,* and *plant sterols*).

- **Nuts and seeds and their oils** (almonds and walnuts) with heart-healthy monounsaturated fatty acids and vitamin E.

- **Whole grains** (quinoa and steel-cut oats) with hearty fibers for cardiovascular and digestive health and calorie control.

## CARBOHYDRATES

Carbohydrates provide calories in the forms of starches and sugars that convert into *glucose*, the body's main dietary source of energy. Carbohydrates vary significantly in their nutritional benefits and relationship to chronic inflammation. They are often classified as *high-glycemic (HG) carbohydrates* and *low-glycemic (HG) carbohydrates* according to how fast they convert into glucose and affect blood sugar levels.

*High-glycemic (HG) carbohydrates* typically have more impact on blood sugar. HG-carbohydrates include cakes, candies, cookies, soft drinks, and processed foods made with white flours. HG-carbohydrates have been connected with increased levels of C-reactive protein, may trigger or worsen chronic inflammation, and add calories.

*Low-glycemic (LG) carbohydrates* tend to digest slowly and generally have less impact on blood sugar. LG-carbohydrates include fresh fruits and vegetables, legumes (dried beans, lentils, and peas), unsweetened dairy products, and whole grains. LG-carbohydrates may also help to reduce or stabilize chronic inflammation.

### for example:

Whole grains are generally LG-carbohydrates that tend to reduce spikes in blood sugar and decrease C-reactive protein levels. The fibers in whole grains may moderate inflammatory processes by promoting weight loss and providing beneficial gut bacteria.

• Whole grains include amaranth, barley, bulgur, einkorn, emmer, farro, kamut, millet, oats (especially steel cut), rye, spelt, teff, triticale, and wheat berries*.

• Some whole grains are considered *"ancient grains"* which mean they have not been modified or crossbred throughout the years*.

• Buckwheat groats (kasha), quinoa, and basmati, brown and wild rice are technically seeds, though often grouped as whole grains, like couscous that is tiny pasta.

*People with diagnosed food allergies may need to eliminate some of these whole and ancient grains.*

**USE:** In general, replace refined HG-carbohydrates with unrefined LG-carbohydrates that provide more antioxidants, fibers, protein, vitamins, and minerals for improved blood sugar control and less chronic inflammation.

**LIMIT:** Natural sugars, such as agave, honey, maple syrup, and molasses with some trace micronutrients. Non-caloric artificial sweeteners (NAS), such as aspartame (Equal), saccharine (Sweet 'n Low), and sucralose (Splenda) may alter GI bacteria and affect how the body handles glucose.

**AVOID:** Sugars, since they tend to spike blood sugar levels and contain more calories than nutrients.

Sugars include those with the suffix "-ose" (such as dextrose, galactose, glucose, lactose, and maltose), as well as barley malt, beet sugar, brown sugar, buttered syrup, cane juice, date sugar, dehydrated cane juice, cane juice solids, cane juice crystals, caramel, carob crystals, carob syrup, corn syrup, corn syrup solids, dehydrated fruit juice, date sugar, diatase, diatastic malt, dextrin, dextran, ethyl maltol, fruit juice, fruit juice concentrate, fruit juice crystals, golden syrup, honey, maltodextrin, malt syrup, maple syrup, Refiner's syrup, sorghum syrup, turbinado sugar, yellow sugar, and others.

Refined grains made with processed white flours should also be avoided.

## GLUTEN INTOLERANCE AND CELIAC DISEASE

**Gluten** is a complex protein that is found in some ancient and whole grains (barley, brewer's yeast, bulgur, couscous, eikorn, emmer, farro, kamut, kasha, malt, matzo meal, oats, rye, spelt, triticale, and wheat). Gluten may trigger *gluten intolerance*, a non-celiac gluten sensitivity.

**Gluten intolerance** is a wheat-related disorder that affects the gastrointestinal tract. Symptoms may include abdominal pain, bloating, diarrhea, nausea and/or gas after consuming foods with wheat. Gluten intolerance is unlike wheat allergy in that the symptoms may not be life-threatening. Treatment focuses on dietary modifications.

**Celiac disease** may damage the small intestine and affect its ability to absorb nutrients, lead to gastrointestinal symptoms (such as abdominal pain, bloating, and diarrhea), and affect other organs and tissues. Conditions such as anemia, headache, depression, fibromyalgia, infertility, miscarriage, joint pain, osteoporosis, and skin rashes may also be connected with gluten intolerance.

Celiac disease may be detected by a blood test that distinguishes *gluten antibodies* (protein markers that are produced by the body's immune system). An endoscopic biopsy may note any changes in the small intestine.

## FRUITS

Whole seasonable fresh fruits are preferred for their rich sources of antioxidant and anti-inflammatory *carotenoids* and *flavonoids*.

### for example:

- **Apples** are high in insoluble and soluble fibers (*pectin*) that may curb appetite, antioxidant vitamins A and C, and polyphenols that may lower levels of cholesterol and C-reactive protein.

- **Berries** contain *anthocyanins*, polyphenol compounds that may moderate inflammation.

- **Cherries** contain *analgesic substances* and *anthocyanins*.

- **Citrus** fruits such as grapefruits, lemons, limes, and oranges contain antioxidant vitamin C and *flavonoids* that may neutralize free radicals.

- **Pineapple** contains *bromelain*, a mixture of enzymes that include *cysteine proteinases* that digest proteins and contribute anti-inflammatory benefits.

- **Watermelon** contains *lycopene*, a carotenoid pigment and phytochemical that may inhibit numerous inflammatory processes and *choline* that may help suppress chronic inflammation.

**USE:** The best anti-inflammatory fruit choices include apples, apricots, bananas, blueberries, blackberries, cherries, cranberries, fresh figs, kiwi, melons, nectarines, oranges, peaches, pears, pink grapefruit, plums, pomegranates, red grapes, and strawberries.

**LIMIT:** Canned or frozen fruits in fruit juice. Additionally, citrus fruits may be limited for people with citrus sensitivities since they may contribute to inflammation under certain conditions.

**AVOID:** Canned or frozen fruits in sugar syrup, dried fruits, and fruit juices packed with added sugars.

## VEGETABLES

Fresh and lightly cooked vegetables are recommended for their antioxidant and anti-inflammatory *carotenoids* and *flavonoids*.

### for example:

**Alliums** such as chives, garlic, leeks, onions, green onions, and shallots contain *organosulfides*, phytochemicals that may boost the immune system, contribute to a healthy gut and lower inflammation.

- **Garlic** contains *diallyl sulfide*, an anti-inflammatory that may limit pro-inflammatory effects of *cytokines* and combat cartilage damage and arthritic pain.

- **Onions** contain *quercetin*, an antioxidant and anti-inflammatory that may inhibit allergic-reactive *histamines*.

**Cruciferous vegetables (crucifers)** such as arugula, bok choy, broccoli, Brussels sprouts, cabbage, cauliflower, collard greens, kale, kohlrabi, mizuna, mustard greens, radish greens, and turnip greens are considered anti-inflammatory superstars.

- Crucifers contain *sulforaphane*, a phytochemical that may block enzymes linked to chronic inflammation and joint deterioration.

- *Sulforaphane* may also prevent or reverse damage to blood vessel linings caused by chronic blood sugar irregularities and inflammation.

**Fermented probiotic vegetables** such as kimchi, pickles, and sauerkraut may improve intestinal flora, increase antibodies and strengthen the immune system.

**Leafy green vegetables** such as kale, lettuce, romaine lettuce, spinach, and Swiss chard contain a rich supply of antioxidant vitamin E that may protect against inflammatory molecules such as *cytokines*.

**Mushrooms (fungi)** such as organic enokitake, maitake, and oyster mushrooms contain antioxidants that may have anti-cancer, anti-inflammatory, and immune-enhancing effects.

**Root vegetables (tubers)** such as beets, carrots, celery root (celeriac), radishes, rutabagas, sweet potatoes, turnips, and winter squash are sources of antioxidants and anti-inflammatory flavonoids.

**Sea vegetables (edible seaweed)** such as arame, brown algae, dulse, kelp, nori, and wakame contain antioxidant *carotenoids* and *polyphenols* and may block pro-inflammatory *cytokines* and other potentially inflammatory substances.

**Other vegetables** such as asparagus and green beans with the flavonoid *quercetin* and other phytonutrients are considered anti-inflammatory.

**USE:** Emphasize these vegetables with their noteworthy anti-inflammatory substances: garlic, onions, broccoli and crucifers, fermented probiotic vegetables (kimchi, pickles, and sauerkraut), romaine lettuce, spinach, and Swiss chard.

**LIMIT:** Nightshade vegetables (bell peppers, chilies, eggplant, potatoes, and tomatoes) that contain *glycoalkaloids*, and natural pesticides associated with some arthritic symptoms that include joint pain. However, some nightshade vegetables contain appreciable amounts of antioxidant vitamins A and C that may combat inflammation.

**AVOID:** Breaded, fried, salted, or sauced vegetables that are higher in calories, refined carbohydrates, sodium, and sugars may provoke inflammation. So may corn, especially if there is allergic cross-reactivity to corn products as found in high-fructose corn syrup (HFCS) sweetened soft drinks.

## FATS AND OILS

The most favorable anti-inflammatory fats and oils are rich in *monounsaturated fatty acids* and/or *omega-3-fatty acids*.

**Monounsaturated fatty acids** found in avocados, nuts, and canola and olive oils, may be protective against cardiovascular disease and certain cancers and may improve insulin sensitivity.

**Omega-3 fatty acids** found in cold-water fish, flaxseeds, omega-3 enriched eggs, walnuts, and whole-soy foods, may inhibit an enzymatic pathway that produces *prostaglandins* that activate pain, trigger inflammation, and defend the body against disease.

In contrast, **omega 6-fatty acids**, found in oils such as corn, safflower, soy, sunflower, and vegetable and their products may trigger the body to produce pro-inflammatory substances.

### for example:

• **Avocados** contain antioxidants, carotenoids (*betacarotene, lutein and zeaxanthin*), mono- and poly-unsaturated fatty acids (including the omega-3 fatty acid *alpha-linolenic*), phytosterols, and *polyhydroxolated fatty alcohols* that may help to reduce elevated blood sugar, cholesterol and inflammation, and lessen the effects of osteo- and rheumatoid arthritis.

• **Nuts and nut "butters"** such as almonds, hazelnuts, and walnuts and their oils are good sources of mono- and polyunsaturated fatty acids (including omega-3 fatty acids and antioxidant vitamin E) that may protect against harmful free radicals and reduce inflammation. Specifically, almonds, hazelnuts, and pecans provide excellent sources of vitamin E.

**(continued)**

• **Oils** such as canola and olive are rich in omega-3 fatty acids. Canola and extra virgin olive oil are mostly comprised of *oleic acid*, a mono-unsaturated fatty acid that is associated with reduced blood pressure and LDL (bad) cholesterol and increased HDL (good) cholesterol. Olive oil is also a rich source of polyphenols with anti-inflammatory and antioxidant properties.

• **Seeds and seed "butters"** that include chia and freshly-ground flaxseeds are high in omega-3 fatty acids and *lignans*, phytochemicals with antioxidant properties. While hemp seeds tend to be higher in omega-6 fatty acids than other seeds, they contain *gamma linoleic acid (GLA)* that is considered anti-inflammatory.

• **Coconut oil** is mostly comprised of saturated fatty acids (as the medium-chain triglyceride *lauric acid*). It is easily digestible and may help increase HDL-cholesterol and deliver anti-inflammatory benefits.

**USE:** Non-GMO canola and olive oil with anti-inflammatory omega-3 fatty acids.

**LIMIT:** Corn, coconut, safflower, sesame, soy, and sunflower oils and hemp seeds with some pro-inflammatory omega-6 fatty acids should be limited.

**AVOID:** Butter, lard and margarine, the skin on poultry, and the fat that surrounds some meats contain saturated fatty acids that may raise total blood cholesterol and LDL (bad) cholesterol. These blood markers are of particular concern for people with arthritis who may also have greater risk of heart disease.

Trans fats may be found in very small amounts in beef and dairy products and some baked goods and fried foods. Most trans fats are formed when hydrogen is added to vegetable oils in the hydrogenation process and may trigger inflammation.

## PROTEINS

Lean proteins may help to stabilize blood sugar and curtail inflammation. Focus on vegetable proteins, especially from legumes and soybeans, fish with omega-3 fatty acids, and vitamin and mineral-rich nuts and seeds. Emphasize fresh protein-rich foods and minimize or eliminate processed proteins and fast foods.

**for example:**

• **Legumes** such as Anasazi, adzuki, black, kidney and navy beans, black-eyed peas, chickpeas, and lentils are rich in folic acid, magnesium, potassium, and soluble fibers that help stabilize blood sugar levels. Legumes are also good-to-excellent sources of B-vitamins, calcium, iron, protein, zinc and phytochemicals that help limit inflammation.

• **Soy foods**—edamame, miso, tempeh, and tofu—contain fibers, polyunsaturated fatty acids, protein, vitamins, and minerals. Soy foods are low in saturated fats and contain *phytosterols* that may help lower LDL-cholesterol.

• **Dairy foods** that are organic and unsweetened, and low- or nonfat may be incorporated as tolerated. Some dairy foods may provoke *lactose intolerance* or *casein sensitivity* with consequential gastrointestinal symptoms.

• **Eggs** such as omega-3-enriched eggs that are laid by hens fed a flax meal-enriched diet, or organic eggs from free-range chickens may be included in an anti-inflammatory protocol if allergies permit.

• **Cheeses** such as Emmental (Swiss), Jarlsberg, and authentic Parmesan that are low- or nonfat may be incorporated as tolerated.

• **Fermented, probiotic dairy products** such as kefir and yogurt with live cultures that are low- or nonfat may promote immunity.

• **Fish** such as anchovies, black cod (sablefish), flounder, halibut, herring, mackerel, wild salmon (especially sockeye), sardines, and tuna are some of the best sources of anti-inflammatory omega-3 fatty acids.

**USE:** Incorporate lower-fat protein sources with their notable anti-inflammatory substances: fermented, probiotic dairy products (especially kefir and yogurt), legumes, and fish (especially sockeye salmon and sardines).

**LIMIT:** Grass-fed, free-range, and organic lean meats (beef, lamb, and pork), and cage-free organic and skinless poultry tend to have higher levels of anti-inflammatory omega-3 fatty acids and lower levels of pro-inflammatory omega-6 fatty acids than protein foods produced other ways. Shellfish that include clams, lobster, oysters, mussels, and scallops tend to be higher in cholesterol and might generate or exacerbate gouty arthritis.

**AVOID:** Bacon, higher-fat cuts of beef such as corned beef, sausages, and spareribs; full-fat dairy products such as butter, cheese, cream, half-and-half, and ice cream; higher-fat foods with saturated and/or trans fatty acids, such as fried chicken or French fries; meats that are not free-range, grass-fed, or organic, processed meats (sandwich meats and sausages), and meat alternatives (veggie burgers and crumbles) may encourage inflammation as may peanuts in allergy-prone individuals.

## FLUIDS

Although acute and chronic inflammation may be accompanied by swelling from the accumulation of body fluids, this does not mean that fluids should be restricted. On the contrary, water has many vital bodily functions. Hydration fights inflammation by flushing toxins out of the body, keeping the joints well-lubricated, and supporting weight loss.

### for example:

**WATER**

• Water carries nutrients and oxygen to and through the blood and maintains water balance, internal body temperature, and moisture.

• Water naturally suppresses the appetite, assists in metabolism of stored body fat, and transports by-products of fat metabolism for disposal.

• Dehydration may lead to dizziness, dry hair, mouth and skin, headaches, increased thirst, decreased urine output and at its worst, confusion, low blood pressure, rapid heart rate, or even coma, seizure, or death.

• At least 8 to 10 (8-ounce) glasses of natural or spring water (or naturally-flavored water) should be consumed daily depending upon individual needs, conditions and disease states, medications, and recommendations of health care providers.

**ALCOHOL**

• The benefits and disadvantages of alcohol consumption are conflicting. On the plus side, some alcoholic beverages (such as red wine with antioxidants) may help to improve insulin sensitivity, raise HDL (good) cholesterol, reduce blood clotting, and improve cardiovascular health.

• Additionally, more highly distilled alcoholic beverages (vodka) contain zero grams of sugar.

• On the negative side, alcohol consumption may be counter-indicated and non-tolerated in certain ethnic populations. For example, some Eastern Asians produce elevated amounts of *acetaldehyde*, a potentially toxic by-product of alcohol metabolism, with side effects that may include flushing, headache, nausea, and higher incidence of esophageal cancer.

**(continued)**

• Also on the negative side are *tannins* in red wine with their astringency that may lead to headaches in some prone individuals.

## COFFEE

• Coffee contains phytochemicals that might reduce inflammation.

• *Caffeine*, a bitter-tasting alkaloid in coffee, is a central nervous system and cardiac stimulator.

• Moderate coffee consumption may be beneficial for cardiovascular health.

• However, coffee contains *tannins* like teas that may produce adverse gastrointestinal effects.

## TEA

• White, green, and oolong teas are rich in *catechins*, antioxidants that may help reduce inflammation.

• In particular, pure green (unfermented) tea leaves generally contain antioxidant-rich *polyphenols*, such as *epigallocatchin gallate*.

• Green tea also contains the alkaloids *caffeine, theophylline*, and *theobromine* that may function as *antimicrobials*, asthma inhibitors, and energy boosters and the amino acid *L-theanine* that is associated with mental acuity and nerve relaxation.

• Sugared beverages such as cocoa, fruit "-ades" such as lemonade, soft drinks, smoothies, sweetened alcoholic drinks, and sweetened coffee and tea mixes may promote inflammation.

• Diet sodas with artificial and natural sweeteners may still induce increased insulin response and may trigger weight gain, increased obesity risks (such as diabetes and heart disease), and other inflammatory conditions.

**USE:** Natural mineral and spring water and water flavored with citrus or natural extracts.

**LIMIT:** Alcohol, coffee and tea as described.

**AVOID:** Sugared beverages and diet sodas as indicated.

## OTHER ANTI-INFLAMMATORY SUBSTANCES

Substances other than those found in major nutrients and water may be helpful in preventing and/or alleviating some inflammation symptoms. In addition to some coffees and teas, these include chocolate and various herbs and spices. Other substances, such as salt, may be sources of inflammation where indicated.

### for example:

#### DARK CHOCOLATE

- Dark chocolate with at least 70 percent cocoa contains antioxidants such as flavonols that may help to reduce inflammation and maintain healthy endothelial cells that line the arteries.

- Dark chocolate may also benefit cardiovascular function by improving arterial blood flow and reducing blood pressure, enhancing insulin sensitivity, and boosting healthy bacteria in the gastrointestinal tract.

#### HERBS AND SPICES

Allspice contains analgesic, anti-bacterial, anti-inflammatory, and antioxidant substances.

- Allspice contains *eugenol*, *quercetin*, and *tannins* that help neutralize free radicals and counteract cellular mutations.

- Allspice might alleviate some arthritis, gout, hemorrhoids, and muscular aches and pains related to injuries and surgical recovery.

Allspice may support dental health and maintain healthy digestion.

**Black pepper** contains *piperine* an alkaloid found in the outer skin of pepper "berries" and jalapeño peppers.

- Piperine may boost the effectiveness of *curcumin* absorption (*see turmeric*).

- Black pepper is commonly used for gastrointestinal motility disorders.

**Cayenne** found in chili peppers contains *capsaicinoids*, alkaloids with pain-reduction and anti-inflammatory properties.

**Cloves** contain antibacterial, anti-inflammatory, and antioxidant benefits.

- Cloves may act as an anti-inflammatory for the mouth and throat, expectorant, and remedy for nausea and upset stomach.

- Cloves contain *kaempferol* and *rhamnetin*, flavonoids with similar properties to *eugenol*, an antiseptic and anti-inflammatory that may protect against cardiovascular disease by inhibiting abnormal blood platelet clotting.

**(continued)**

**Cinnamon** contains *cinnamaldehyde*, a compound that may inhibit certain pro-inflammatory proteins and prevent blood platelet clotting.

- Cinnamon may help activate insulin receptors that assist blood sugar control.

- Cinnamon might block growth factors that are involved in abnormal cell growth and may be protective against certain cancers.

**Ginger** contains antioxidant vitamin C, *gingerol* and *shogoal*, phenols that may help block inflammatory pathways.

- Ginger may act as an intestinal spasmolytic that relaxes and soothes the intestinal tract.

- Ginger might also help reduce some osteoarthritis symptoms as a pain reliever and some side effects associated with chemotherapy.

**Marjoram** contains vitamins A, C, and K and may contain analgesic, anti-inflammatory, and antioxidant properties.

- Marjoram may support bone health and help reduce pain associated with arthritis, colds, fevers, headaches, muscular overexertion, spasms, and toothaches.

- Marjoram might also improve digestion by stimulating digestive enzymes.

**Nutmeg** contains pain-relieving properties from its volatile oils that include *elemicin*, *eugenol*, *myristicin*, and *safrole*.

- Nutmeg may help calm the digestive and nervous systems due to its B-vitamins, calcium, copper, iron, magnesium, manganese, and potassium content.

- Nutmeg might also aid blood pressure regulation and heart function.

**Parsley** contains rich sources of antioxidants and flavonoids.

- Parsley is an excellent source of vitamin C and a good source of vitamin A (notably from its beta-carotene content) and folic acid, an important B-vitamin for its anti-inflammatory properties for arthritis control and cardiovascular health.

- The flavonoids in parsley, particularly *luteolin*, may combat oxygen radicals to thwart cellular damage and increase the antioxidant capacity of the blood.

**Rosemary** contains anti-bacterial, anti-fungal, anti-inflammatory, antioxidant, and antiseptic properties.

**Oregano** contains *betacaryophyllin* that may help inhibit inflammation, resist bowel inflammation associated with Crohn's disease, and prevent bone degeneration associated with osteoarthritis.

**(continued)**

**Sage** contains *carnosic acid* and *carnosol*, two anti-inflammatories that fight inflammation associated with certain neurological conditions and *camphor* that may help destroy bacteria, fungi, and other compounds that may be effective antivirals.

**Thyme** contains *carvacrol*, a phenol that may suppress inflammatory enzymes, inhibit oxidative damage, and improve aches and muscles soreness. Thyme may also function as an antibacterial, antibiotic, antihistamine, and antiphylactic.

**Turmeric,** a member of the ginger family, contains the phenol *curcuminoid*, most important which is *curcumin* with antioxidant and anti-inflammatory effects.

> • Turmeric may be effective in reducing inflammation associated with arthritis and diabetes and in some cancer prevention.

• Turmeric might also be used to treat bronchitis, diabetes and laryngitis; however certain conditions and/or disease states may limit its usage.

**SALT**

While sodium (a component of table salt) is an essential mineral in the human body for muscle contraction and relaxation, electrolyte balance, and nerve transmittance, too much sodium is counter-indicated for inflammation. When the kidneys cannot eliminate sodium effectively or speedily, sodium may accumulate in the blood stream, increase blood pressure, and stress the heart, kidneys, and liver.

Excess sodium may also exacerbate certain inflammatory conditions, such as arthritis, that may cause blood vessels to expand and place pressure on surrounding joints. Corticosteroids used to treat rheumatoid arthritis may add to sodium retention, so excess salt may complicate their use.

**USE:** Dark chocolate and herbs and spices as indicated.

**LIMIT:** Chilies, salt, and other herbs or spices as cautioned.

**AVOID:** Food colorings may trigger allergic reactions and other immune responses. Synthetic colorant molecules are small and the immune system may find them difficult to discern and defend. Colorants may also bind to food or proteins in the body and evade or disrupt the immune system.

## SUPPLEMENTS AND MEDICATIONS

Ideally, dietary management should be able to alleviate and maybe dismiss some inflammatory symptoms. However, some people may have certain medical conditions that may require additional therapies. Some supplements and medications may be effectively integrated into anti-inflammatory treatment plans. These should be individualized according to dietary and medical needs and monitored by health care practitioners.

# anti-inflammatory "know-how"

Switching to an anti-inflammatory diet may seem overwhelming with all of the foods and beverages that should be used, limited, or avoided. Instead, think of an anti-inflammatory diet as a healthy approach to foods and beverages—one that may have been around for ages but has recently come to realization.

The premise of an anti-inflammatory diet is a whole-foods Mediterranean-type dietary approach to eating and drinking with healthy dietary choices that include:

- **Antioxidant and anti-inflammatory-rich herbs and spices** such as black pepper, ginger, and turmeric.

- **Chronic disease-fighting supportive substances** such as dark chocolate and red wine in moderation.

- **Healthful fats with monounsaturated and omega-3 fatty acids** such as avocados, fatty fish, and olive oil.

- **Fiber-rich whole and ancient grains** such as brown rice, quinoa, and steel-cut oats.

- **Immunity-protective pre-and probiotics** such as fermented foods that include kefir, pickled foods, and yogurt.

- **Sugar-free and antioxidant-rich beverages** such as coffees, teas, and natural mineral and spring waters.

- **Vitamin and mineral-rich fruits and vegetables** such as berries, citrus fruits, broccoli, and onions.

## MAKE SMART FOOD AND BEVERAGE CHOICES

Use the dietary advice found in this introduction to make wise food and beverage selections. Focus on foods and beverages that are designated to **USE**, curb foods and beverages that are noted to **LIMIT**, and try to exclude the foods and beverages and other substances that are flagged to **AVOID**. These foods and beverages are color-coded to help make your choices easier. Some ingredients to **LIMIT** are used in small amounts in the recipes throughout this book. Individual tolerance may dictate their use.

## KEEP AN ANTI-INFLAMMATORY KITCHEN

A well-stocked kitchen that supports an anti-inflammatory diet is essential for effective, healthy, and quick meals and snacks. The **USE**, **LIMIT** and **AVOID** guidelines should be your guide. Some items to **LIMIT** are provided for convenience purposes. Pantry staples include those that are shelf-stable. Refrigerated items should be regularly checked for "use by dates".

### pantry

**Broth** (poultry and vegetable)

**Canned fish** (salmon, sardines, and tuna in water, vinegar, and/or oil, without sugars)

**Canned legumes** (beans, peas, and/or lentils, and soy, without sugars)

**Carob powder**

**Chilies**

**Coffee**

**Fermented vegetables** (kimchi, pickles, and sauerkraut)

**Garlic, ginger, and onion powder**

**Kosher and sea salt**

**Mustard** (without sugars)

**Nut and seeds** (almond, cashew, hazelnut, sesame, sunflower, and walnut)

**Nut and seed "butters"** (without sugars)

**Nut and seed flours**

**Vinegar** (apple cider, rice, and wine)

**Peppercorns**

**Herbs** (marjoram, parsley, oregano, rosemary, sage, and thyme)

**Spices** (allspice, black and cayenne pepper, cinnamon, nutmeg, and turmeric)

**Tea**

**Tomato products** (without sugars)

**Unsweetened cocoa powder**

**Whole and ancient grains** (amaranth, barley, bulgur, einkorn, emmer, farro, kamut, millet, oats (especially steel cut), rye, spelt, teff, triticale, and wheat berries)

**Whole grain flour** (flour made from whole grains shown above)

**Water** (natural or spring or naturally flavored, without sugar)

**Wine** (organic red, without sulfites)

### refrigerator

**Cheese** (low- or nonfat Emmental [Swiss], Jarlsberg, and Parmesan)

**Mustards** (without sugar)

**Organic eggs**

**Organic fresh herbs** (chives, marjoram, parsley, oregano, rosemary, sage, and thyme)

**Organic fresh fruit** (avocados, berries, citrus fruits, melons, stone fruits [peaches, pears, and plums], and tropical fruits [kiwi and papaya])

**Organic oil** (avocado, coconut, flax, grape seed, hemp, olive, sesame, and walnut)

**Organic protein** (grass-fed beef, free-range chicken, eggs, cold-water fish, lamb, pork, and turkey)

**Fermented dairy products** (kefir, pickles, and yogurt)

**Salmon and other fatty fish** (anchovies, mackerel, sardines, trout, and tuna)

**Sea vegetables** (dulse, kelp, nori, and wakame)

**Soy** (tempeh and tofu)

**Unsalted nuts, seeds, and nut and seed butters** (almonds, Brazil nuts, cashews, Macadamia nuts, walnuts and chia, ground flax, pumpkin, sesame, and sunflower seeds, and tahini [sesame seed paste])

**Vegetables** (asparagus, beets, bok choy, broccoli, Brussels sprouts, cabbage, carrots, cauliflower, collard greens, cucumbers, dandelion greens, endive, escarole, garlic, ginger, green beans, kale, kohlrabi, leeks, mushrooms, mustard greens, okra, onions, parsley, peas, radishes, romaine and other deep leafy green lettuce, rutabaga, green onions, spinach, sprouts, summer squash, sweet potatoes, Swiss chard, watercress, and zucchini).

## PLAN AND PREPARE FOODS WITH AN ANTI-INFLAMMATORY MINDSET

Here's a chance to focus your planning, shopping, and cooking habits to transpose your diet into an anti-inflammatory eating and drinking plan.

To begin, look at your "normal" weekdays and weekends and which meals you intend to eat in or out. Then divide these meals into composed meals or snacks that match your lifestyle.

In general, it is best to have three balanced meals daily with mini-snacks to help manage your blood sugar and weight. Balancing meals around vitamin and mineral-rich vegetables and fruits, lean proteins, hearty carbohydrates, and healthy fats are a good starting point. Make vegetables a prominent feature of most meals. Fresh ingredients are usually best.

The recipes in this book are designed to maximize anti-inflammatory ingredients and minimize pro-inflammatory foods and beverages.

## examples of recipes that feature anti-inflammatory ingredients include:

- **Butternut Squash and Millet Soup** (with curry powder and millet)

- **Miso Soup with Tofu** (with green onions and seaweed)

- **Roast Sesame Fish** (with sesame oil and seeds and wasabi)

- **Mediterranean Vegetable Bake** (with red onion and rosemary)

- **Vegetarian Quinoa Chili** (with jalapeño pepper and kidney beans)

- **Brown Rice & Vegetable Stuffed Squash** (with brown rice and almonds)

- **Spicy Grapefruit Salad with Raspberry Dressing** (with raspberries and watercress)

- **Spinach Salad with Pomegranate Vinaigrette** (with olive oil and walnuts)

- **Cranberry Fruit Salad** (with grapefruit and oranges)

- **Blueberry Haze** (with apples and ginger)

## SEEK FARM-RAISED, GRASS-FED, IN-SEASON, ORGANIC FOODS AND BEVERAGES

Farm-raised, grass-fed, in-season, organic foods and beverages have gone mainstream at large and small markets and online. Ensure that their sources are accurate and reliable. Purchase staples that are devoid of sugars and other pro-inflammatory substances when they are on sale. Watch for weekly sales of anti-inflammatory protein foods and freeze in portion-controlled amounts. If you purchase extra fresh fruits, herbs, and/or vegetables, they may be "repurposed" into compotes, dressings, salads, sauces, soups, stews, and other preparations.

## DECIPHER FOOD AND NUTRITION LABELS

Food and nutrition labels are meant to assist anti-inflammatory food and beverage selections, not to create alarm. In general, **AVOID** labeling terms that end with "-ose" and other sugar-like substances.

The term "gluten-free" on food labels means that products still have less than 20 ppm of gluten. Watch out for barley, brewer's yeast, malt, oats, rye, triticale, and wheat even if they are labeled "gluten-free" and for the term "wheat-free" that may contain other undesirable and possibly disagreeable substances.

## EAT, DRINK, AND ACT MINDFULLY

Mindful eating is important for any type of diet—especially those that require specific foods and beverages. Mindful and effective anti-inflammatory eating and drinking advocates that you:

- **Plan ahead** for fitting anti-inflammatory foods and beverages.

- **Shop wisely** for fresh and mostly unprocessed foods and beverages.

- **Chart eating plans** that synchronize with lifestyle needs.

- **Maintain healthy meal and snack patterns** to normalize blood sugar.

- **Prepare foods and beverages** that focus on tolerated ingredients.

- **Store pantry and refrigerated items** separately from pro-inflammatory items.

- **Clean and reorganize** an anti-inflammatory pantry and refrigerator.

It's also important to eat and drink mindfully to help alleviate stressful eating. Slow down and enjoy dining experiences. Place silverware down between bites and sip, don't gulp beverages. Chew and swallow food well and try to avoid "downing" food with liquids. Meals and snacks that are consumed on-the-run may not be best for proper digestion. Chronic stressful eating along with everyday pressures may overstress cortisol levels that may increase inflammation.

By keeping a good accounting of what is consumed; for example, what feels good, what doesn't and for what reasons, a person may be able to personalize an anti-inflammatory meal plan. Some measurable time may be needed for the body to adjust and everyday might not be perfect, but inflammatory symptoms may improve day-by-day.

## LIVE AN ANTI-INFLAMMATORY LIFESTYLE

Napping, resting and sleeping, mindful meditation, and regular physical activity may help control stress hormones. So may the elimination or restriction of alcohol and smoking. While some supplements or medications may prove productive, watch out for interactions or overconsumption. Health care advice should be sought and followed.

## SEEK ADDITIONAL HELP, IF NEEDED

Before the start of an anti-inflammatory diet program, a medical and nutritional team with a Registered Dietitian/Nutritionist should be consulted. A Registered Dietitian/Nutritionist is trained in diet and nutrition and counseling and may also be able to evaluate activity and exercise, dietary supplements, and weight.

## SEE A HEALTH CARE PROFESSIONAL, IF NECESSARY

If there are concerning emotional, mental, or physical changes after beginning a anti-inflammatory diet program, a specialized health care professional should be contacted.

Otherwise, most anti-inflammatory foods and beverages may be "just what the doctor ordered" and offer some relief and optimism through healthier food and beverage choices.

# small
# BITES

## avocado salsa

MAKES 32 SERVINGS (ABOUT 4 CUPS)

1 medium avocado, diced

1 cup chopped onion

1 cup peeled seeded chopped cucumber

1 Anaheim pepper,* seeded and chopped

½ cup chopped fresh tomato

2 tablespoons chopped fresh cilantro, plus additional for garnish

½ teaspoon salt

¼ teaspoon hot pepper sauce

*Anaheim peppers can sting and irritate the skin, so wear rubber gloves when handling peppers and do not touch your eyes.*

Combine avocado, onion, cucumber, Anaheim pepper, tomato, 2 tablespoons cilantro, salt and hot pepper sauce in medium bowl; mix gently. Cover and refrigerate at least 1 hour before serving. Garnish with additional cilantro.

# breakfast bites

MAKES 8 SERVINGS

⅔ cup whole wheat pastry flour

⅓ cup buckwheat flour

1 teaspoon baking powder

1 teaspoon sugar

1 teaspoon ground cinnamon

¼ teaspoon salt

2 eggs

¼ to ⅓ cup water

1 teaspoon vanilla

Plain nonfat yogurt and fresh raspberries

**1.** Mix pastry flour, buckwheat flour, baking powder, sugar, cinnamon and salt in medium bowl. Beat eggs, ¼ cup water and vanilla in another medium bowl until smooth. Whisk egg mixture into flour mixture, adding additional water 1 teaspoon at a time as needed, to make a thick batter.

**2.** Heat nonstick skillet or griddle. Drop about 2 tablespoons batter per pancake into skillet. Cook 2 to 3 minutes or until browned and puffy. Flip and cook another 2 to 3 minutes.

**3.** To serve, top each pancake with yogurt and raspberries.

# red pepper relish

MAKES 4 SERVINGS

2 large red bell peppers, cut into thin strips

1 small Vidalia or other sweet onion, thinly sliced

3 tablespoons cider vinegar

1 tablespoon packed light brown sugar

1 tablespoon olive oil

1 tablespoon honey

¼ teaspoon salt

¼ teaspoon dried thyme

¼ teaspoon red pepper flakes

¼ teaspoon black pepper

## slow cooker directions

Combine all ingredients in slow cooker; mix well. Cover; cook on LOW 4 hours.

# roasted sweet potato and hoisin lettuce wraps

1 to 2 large sweet potatoes (about ¾ pound), cut into ½-inch cubes

1 large onion, cut into 8 wedges

1 tablespoon olive oil

Hoisin Dressing (recipe follows)

12 large Bibb lettuce leaves, rinsed and patted dry

2 cups shredded cabbage or packaged coleslaw

½ cup matchstick or shredded carrots

½ cup toasted peanuts (optional)

**1.** Preheat oven to 425°F. Line baking sheet with foil. Place potatoes and onion on baking sheet. Drizzle with oil and toss to coat. Roast 20 minutes or until edges of onion begin to brown and potatoes are tender, stirring once halfway through cooking time.

**2.** Meanwhile, prepare Hoisin Dressing; set aside.

**3.** To serve, top each lettuce leaf with cabbage, sweet potato mixture and carrots. Drizzle with 1 tablespoon dressing and sprinkle with peanuts, if desired. Fold bottom over filling, then fold two sides up to form bundles.

## hoisin dressing

MAKES ABOUT ¾ CUP DRESSING

¼ cup water

¼ cup almond butter

3 tablespoons hoisin sauce

2 tablespoons lime juice

3 cloves garlic, minced

1 tablespoon vegetable oil

1 tablespoon ketchup

2 teaspoons grated fresh ginger

⅛ teaspoon red pepper flakes

Whisk all ingredients in small bowl until well blended.

# mini turkey loaves

1 pound lean ground turkey
1 small apple, chopped
½ small onion, chopped
½ cup old-fashioned oats
2 teaspoons Dijon mustard
1 teaspoon dried rosemary
1 teaspoon salt
Dash black pepper
Cranberry sauce
Vegetable Stir-Fry (recipe follows)
Mashed potatoes (optional)

**1.** Preheat oven to 425°F. Spray 12 standard (2½-inch) muffin cups with nonstick cooking spray.

**2.** Combine turkey, apple, onion, oats, mustard, rosemary, salt and pepper in large bowl; mix just until blended. Press evenly into prepared muffin cups.

**3.** Bake 20 minutes or until lightly browned and cooked through (165°F). Top with cranberry sauce.

**4.** Prepare Vegetable Stir-Fry. Serve with Vegetable Stir-Fry and mashed potatoes, if desired.

## vegetable stir-fry

1 tablespoon olive oil
3 to 4 carrots, diagonally sliced
2 zucchini, diagonally sliced
3 tablespoons orange juice
Salt and black pepper

Heat oil in medium skillet or wok over medium heat. Add carrots; stir-fry 3 minutes. Add zucchini and orange juice; stir-fry 4 minutes or until vegetables are crisp-tender. Season with salt and pepper.

# mini spinach frittatas

## MAKES 12 MINI FRITTATAS

1 tablespoon olive oil

½ cup chopped onion

8 eggs

¼ cup plain nonfat yogurt

1 package (10 ounces) frozen chopped spinach, thawed and squeezed dry

½ cup (2 ounces) shredded reduced-fat Cheddar cheese

¼ cup grated Parmesan cheese

¾ teaspoon salt

⅛ teaspoon black pepper

⅛ teaspoon ground red pepper

Dash ground nutmeg

**1.** Preheat oven to 350°F. Spray 12 standard (2½-inch) muffin cups with nonstick cooking spray.

**2.** Heat oil in large nonstick skillet over medium heat. Add onion; cook and stir about 5 minutes or until tender. Set aside to cool slightly.

**3.** Whisk eggs and yogurt in large bowl. Stir in spinach, Cheddar, Parmesan, salt, black pepper, ground red pepper, nutmeg and onion until blended. Divide mixture evenly among prepared muffin cups.

**4.** Bake 20 to 25 minutes or until eggs are puffed and firm and no longer shiny. Cool in pan 2 minutes. Loosen bottom and sides with small spatula or knife; remove to wire rack. Serve warm, cold or at room temperature.

# monterey potato hash

MAKES 4 TO 6 SERVINGS

4 to 6 cherry tomatoes

2 tablespoons olive oil

4 small baking potatoes, unpeeled and cut into ¼-inch slices

1 medium red onion, sliced

2 cloves garlic, minced

1 teaspoon dried basil or oregano

¼ teaspoon salt

¼ teaspoon black pepper

1 cup water

1 large green bell pepper, halved and cut into ¼-inch slices

¼ cup (1 ounce) shredded low-fat mozzarella or Cheddar cheese

**1.** Rinse tomatoes and pat dry with paper towels. Cut tomatoes in half; set aside.

**2.** Heat wok or large skillet over high heat about 1 minute. Drizzle oil into wok and heat 30 seconds. Add potatoes; cook about 8 minutes or until lightly browned, stirring often. Reduce heat to medium. Add onion, garlic, basil, salt and black pepper; stir-fry 1 minute.

**3.** Stir in water; cover and cook 5 minutes or until potatoes are fork-tender, gently stirring once. Add bell pepper; stir-fry until water evaporates. Gently stir in tomatoes; cook until heated through. Transfer to serving dish; sprinkle with cheese.

# soups &
# STEWS

## miso soup with tofu

MAKES 4 (1 CUP) SERVINGS

4 cups water

1 tablespoon shredded nori or wakame seaweed

8 ounces firm tofu

3 green onions, finely chopped

¼ cup white miso

2 teaspoons reduced-sodium soy sauce

**1.** Bring water to a simmer in medium saucepan. Add nori; simmer 6 minutes.

**2.** Meanwhile, press tofu between paper towels to remove excess water. Cut into ½-inch cubes.

**3.** Reduce heat to low. Add tofu, green onions, miso and soy sauce; cook and stir until miso is dissolved and soup is heated through. (Do not boil.)

# italian skillet roasted vegetable soup

MAKES 5 SERVINGS

2 tablespoons olive oil, divided

1 medium orange, red or yellow bell pepper, chopped

1 clove garlic, minced

2 cups water

1 can (about 14 ounces) diced tomatoes

1 medium zucchini, thinly sliced lengthwise

⅛ teaspoon red pepper flakes

1 can (about 15 ounces) navy beans, rinsed and drained

3 to 4 tablespoons chopped fresh basil

1 tablespoon balsamic vinegar

¾ teaspoon salt

½ teaspoon liquid smoke (optional)

**1.** Heat 1 tablespoon oil in Dutch oven over medium-high heat. Add bell pepper; cook and stir 4 minutes or until edges are browned. Add garlic; cook and stir 15 seconds. Add water, tomatoes, zucchini and red pepper flakes; bring to a boil over high heat. Reduce heat to low; cover and simmer 20 minutes.

**2.** Add beans, basil, remaining 1 tablespoon oil, vinegar, salt and liquid smoke, if desired; simmer 5 minutes. Remove from heat; let stand, covered, 10 minutes before serving.

# hot and sour soup
# with bok choy and tofu

MAKES 4 SERVINGS

1 tablespoon dark sesame oil

4 ounces fresh shiitake mushrooms, stems finely chopped, caps thinly sliced

2 cloves garlic, minced

2 cups mushroom broth or vegetable broth

1 cup plus 2 tablespoons cold water, divided

2 tablespoons reduced-sodium soy sauce

1½ tablespoons rice vinegar or white wine vinegar

¼ teaspoon red pepper flakes

1½ tablespoons cornstarch

2 cups coarsely chopped bok choy leaves or napa cabbage

10 ounces silken extra firm tofu, well drained, cut into ½-inch cubes

1 green onion, thinly sliced

**1.** Heat oil in large saucepan over medium heat. Add mushrooms and garlic; cook and stir 3 minutes. Add broth, 1 cup water, soy sauce, vinegar and red pepper flakes; bring to a boil. Simmer 5 minutes.

**2.** Whisk remaining 2 tablespoons water into cornstarch in small bowl until smooth. Stir into soup; simmer 2 minutes or until thickened. Stir in bok choy; simmer 2 to 3 minutes or until wilted. Stir in tofu; heat through. Ladle soup into bowls; sprinkle with green onion.

# slow cooker veggie stew

## MAKES 4 TO 6 SERVINGS

1 tablespoon olive oil

⅔ cup carrot slices

½ cup diced onion

2 cloves garlic, chopped

2 cans (about 14 ounces each) vegetable broth

1½ cups chopped green cabbage

½ cup cut green beans

½ cup diced zucchini

1 tablespoon tomato paste

½ teaspoon dried basil

½ teaspoon dried oregano

¼ teaspoon salt

### slow cooker directions

**1.** Heat oil in medium skillet over medium-high heat. Add carrot, onion and garlic; cook and stir until tender. Transfer to slow cooker.

**2.** Stir in remaining ingredients. Cover; cook on LOW 8 to 10 hours or on HIGH 4 to 5 hours.

# cannellini bean stew with roasted tomatoes & zucchini

4 plum tomatoes

4 teaspoons olive oil, divided

1 small onion, chopped

2 cloves garlic, minced

2 cans (about 15 ounces each) cannellini beans, rinsed and drained

2 medium zucchini, cut into ½-inch cubes

2 cups fat-free reduced-sodium vegetable broth

¼ teaspoon salt

½ teaspoon dried basil

¼ teaspoon black pepper

**1.** Preheat broiler. Spray baking pan with nonstick cooking spray.

**2.** Cut tomatoes in half lengthwise; place, cut side up, on baking pan. Drizzle with 2 teaspoons oil; broil 12 minutes or until well browned. Let tomatoes cool slightly. Transfer tomatoes to food processor; process using on/off pulsing action or until coarsely chopped.

**3.** Meanwhile, heat remaining 2 teaspoons oil in large saucepan over medium-high heat. Cook and stir onion 3 minutes. Add garlic; cook and stir 1 minute. Add beans, zucchini, broth, tomatoes and salt. Bring to a boil. Reduce heat and simmer, covered, 8 minutes or just until zucchini is tender. Stir in basil and pepper.

# chilled cucumber soup

MAKES 4 SERVINGS

1 large cucumber, peeled and coarsely chopped

¾ cup silken tofu or dairy-free sour cream

¼ cup packed fresh dill

½ teaspoon salt

⅛ teaspoon ground white pepper

1½ cups vegetable broth

Sprigs fresh dill

**1.** Place cucumber in food processor; process until finely chopped. Add sour cream, ¼ cup dill, salt and pepper; process until fairly smooth.

**2.** Transfer mixture to large bowl; stir in broth. Cover and chill at least 2 hours or up to 24 hours. Ladle into shallow bowls; garnish with dill sprigs.

# chicken soup au pistou

MAKES 8 SERVINGS

½ pound boneless skinless chicken breasts, cut into ½-inch pieces

1 large onion, diced

3 cans (about 14 ounces each) chicken broth

1 can (about 15 ounces) Great Northern beans, rinsed and drained

1 can (about 14 ounces) whole tomatoes, undrained

2 carrots, sliced

1 large potato, diced

¼ teaspoon salt

¼ teaspoon black pepper

1 cup fresh or frozen green beans, cut into 1-inch pieces

¼ cup pesto

Grated Parmesan cheese (optional)

**1.** Spray large saucepan with olive oil cooking spray; heat over medium-high heat. Add chicken; cook and stir 5 minutes or until browned. Add onion; cook and stir 2 minutes.

**2.** Add broth, Great Northern beans, tomatoes, carrots, potato, salt and pepper. Bring to a boil, stirring to break up tomatoes. Reduce heat to low. Cover and simmer 15 minutes, stirring occasionally. Add green beans; cook 5 minutes or until vegetables are tender.

**3.** Ladle soup into bowls. Top each serving with 1½ teaspoons pesto and sprinkle with Parmesan cheese, if desired.

# butternut squash and millet soup

## MAKES 6 SERVINGS

1 red bell pepper

1 teaspoon olive oil

2¼ cups diced butternut squash *or* 1 package (10 ounces) frozen diced butternut squash

1 medium red onion, chopped

1 teaspoon curry powder

½ teaspoon smoked paprika

½ teaspoon salt

⅛ teaspoon black pepper

2 cups low-sodium chicken broth

2 boneless skinless chicken breasts (about 4 ounces each), cooked and chopped

1 cup cooked millet

**1.** Place bell pepper on rack in broiler pan 3 to 5 inches from heat source or hold over open gas flame on long-handled metal fork. Turn bell pepper often until blistered and charred on all sides. Transfer to resealable food storage bag; seal bag and let stand 15 to 20 minutes to loosen skin. Remove loosened skin with paring knife. Cut off top and scrape out seeds; discard.

**2.** Heat oil in large saucepan over high heat. Add squash, bell pepper and onion; cook and stir 5 minutes. Add curry powder, paprika, salt and black pepper. Pour in broth; bring to a boil. Cover and cook 7 to 10 minutes or until vegetables are tender.

**3.** Purée soup in saucepan with hand-held immersion blender or in batches in food processor or blender. Return soup to saucepan. Stir in chicken and millet; cook until heated through.

# italian escarole and white bean stew

MAKES 4 SERVINGS

1 tablespoon olive oil

1 onion, chopped

3 carrots, cut into ½-inch-thick rounds

2 cloves garlic, minced

1 can (about 14 ounces) vegetable broth

1 head escarole (about 12 ounces)

¼ teaspoon red pepper flakes

2 cans (about 15 ounces each) Great Northern white beans, rinsed and drained

Salt

Grated Parmesan cheese (optional)

## slow cooker directions

**1.** Heat oil in medium skillet over medium-high heat. Add onion and carrots; cook and stir about 5 minutes or until onion is softened. Add garlic; cook and stir 1 minute. Transfer to slow cooker. Pour in broth.

**2.** Trim base of escarole. Roughly cut crosswise into 1-inch-wide strips. Wash well in large bowl of cold water. Lift out by handfuls, leaving sand or dirt in bottom of bowl. Shake to remove excess water, but do not dry. Add to slow cooker. Sprinkle with red pepper flakes. Top with beans.

**3.** Cover; cook on LOW 7 to 8 hours or on HIGH 3½ to 4 hours or until escarole is wilted and very tender. Season with salt. Serve in bowls and sprinkle with Parmesan, if desired.

**tip:** Escarole is very leafy and easily fills a 4½-quart slow cooker when raw, but it shrinks dramatically as it cooks down. This recipe makes 4 portions, but can easily be doubled. Simply double the quantities of all the ingredients listed and be sure to use a 6-quart (or larger) slow cooker.

# vegetarian chili

MAKES 4 SERVINGS

1 tablespoon olive oil

1 cup finely chopped onion

1 cup chopped red bell pepper

2 tablespoons minced jalapeño pepper*

1 clove garlic, minced

1 can (28 ounces) crushed tomatoes

1 can (about 15 ounces) black beans, rinsed and drained

1 can (about 15 ounces) chickpeas, rinsed and drained

½ cup corn

¼ cup tomato paste

1 teaspoon sugar

1 teaspoon ground cumin

1 teaspoon dried basil

1 teaspoon chili powder

¼ teaspoon black pepper

Sour cream and shredded Cheddar cheese (optional)

*Jalapeño peppers can sting and irritate the skin, so wear rubber gloves when handling peppers and do not touch your eyes.

## slow cooker directions

**1.** Heat oil in large nonstick skillet over medium-high heat until hot. Add onion, bell pepper, jalapeño pepper and garlic; cook and stir 5 minutes or until tender.

**2.** Transfer onion mixture to slow cooker. Add remaining ingredients except sour cream and cheese; mix well. Cover; cook on LOW 4 to 5 hours.

**3.** Garnish with sour cream and cheese, if desired.

# main-dish salads
# & ENTRÉES

## gazpacho shrimp salad

MAKES 4 SERVINGS

½ cup chunky salsa

1 tablespoon balsamic vinegar

1 tablespoon extra virgin olive oil

1 clove garlic, minced

8 cups torn mixed salad greens or romaine lettuce

1 large tomato, chopped

1 small ripe avocado, diced

½ cup thinly sliced unpeeled cucumber

½ pound large cooked shrimp, peeled and deveined

½ cup coarsely chopped fresh cilantro

**1.** Combine salsa, vinegar, oil and garlic in small bowl; mix well.

**2.** Combine greens, tomato, avocado and cucumber in large bowl. Divide salad among 4 plates; top with shrimp. Drizzle dressing over salads; sprinkle with cilantro.

# roasted salmon with new potatoes and red onions

## MAKES 6 SERVINGS

¼ cup reduced-sodium chicken broth

1 tablespoon olive oil

1½ pounds small new potatoes, cut into halves

1 medium red onion, cut into ¼-inch-thick wedges

6 salmon fillets (4 ounces each)

½ teaspoon black pepper

Sprigs fresh tarragon or dill (optional)

**1.** Preheat oven to 400°F. Spray large shallow roasting pan or jelly-roll pan with nonstick cooking spray.

**2.** Combine broth and oil in small bowl. Combine potatoes and half of broth mixture in prepared pan; toss to coat. Roast 20 minutes.

**3.** Add onion and remaining broth mixture to pan; toss to coat. Push vegetables to edges of pan; place salmon in center. Sprinkle salmon and vegetables with pepper. Roast 10 to 15 minutes or until center of salmon is opaque and vegetables are tender. Garnish with tarragon.

# greek chicken & spinach rice casserole

MAKES 4 SERVINGS

1   cup finely chopped onion

1   package (10 ounces)
    frozen chopped spinach,
    thawed and squeezed dry

1   cup uncooked quick-
    cooking brown rice

1   cup water

¼   teaspoon salt

⅛   teaspoon ground red
    pepper

¾   pound chicken tenders

2   teaspoons Greek
    seasoning (oregano,
    rosemary and sage
    mixture)

½   teaspoon salt-free lemon-
    pepper seasoning

1   tablespoon olive oil

1   lemon, cut into wedges

**1.** Preheat oven to 350°F. Spray large ovenproof skillet with nonstick cooking spray; heat over medium heat. Add onion; cook and stir 2 minutes or until translucent. Add spinach, rice, water, salt and ground red pepper. Stir until well blended. Remove from heat.

**2.** Place chicken on top of mixture in skillet in single layer. Sprinkle with Greek seasoning and lemon-pepper seasoning. Cover with foil. Bake 25 minutes or until chicken is no longer pink in center.

**3.** Remove foil. Drizzle oil evenly over top. Serve with lemon wedges.

# mandarin chicken salad

MAKES 4 SERVINGS

3½ ounces thin rice noodles (rice vermicelli)

1 can (6 ounces) mandarin orange segments, chilled

⅓ cup honey

2 tablespoons rice wine vinegar

2 tablespoons reduced-sodium soy sauce

1 can (8 ounces) sliced water chestnuts, drained

4 cups shredded napa cabbage

1 cup shredded red cabbage

½ cup sliced radishes

4 thin slices red onion, cut in half and separated

3 boneless skinless chicken breasts (about 12 ounces), cooked and cut into strips

**1.** Place rice noodles in large bowl. Cover with hot water; soak 20 minutes or until soft. Drain.

**2.** Drain mandarin orange segments, reserving ⅓ cup liquid. Whisk reserved liquid, honey, vinegar and soy sauce in medium bowl. Add water chestnuts.

**3.** Divide noodles, cabbages, radishes and onion evenly among 4 serving plates. Top with chicken and orange segments. Remove water chestnuts from dressing and arrange on salads. Serve with remaining dressing.

# cedar plank salmon with grilled citrus mango

MAKES 4 SERVINGS

4 salmon fillets (6 ounces each), skin intact

1 teaspoon chili powder

½ teaspoon black pepper

¼ teaspoon salt

¼ teaspoon ground allspice

2 tablespoons orange juice

1 tablespoon lemon juice

1 tablespoon lime juice

2 teaspoons minced fresh ginger

¼ cup chopped fresh mint

⅛ teaspoon red pepper flakes

2 medium mangoes, peeled and cut into 1-inch pieces

1 cedar plank (about 15×7 inches, ½ inch thick), soaked*

*Soak in water 5 hours or overnight.

**1.** Prepare grill for direct cooking over medium-high heat.

**2.** Rinse and pat dry salmon fillets. Combine chili powder, black pepper, salt and allspice in small bowl. Rub evenly over flesh side of fillets. Set aside.

**3.** Combine orange, lemon and lime juices, ginger, mint and red pepper flakes in medium bowl; mix well.

**4.** Thread mango pieces onto skewers or spread out in grill basket.

**5.** If using charcoal grill, wait until coals are covered with gray ash to start grilling salmon. If using gas grill, turn heat down to medium. Keep clean spray bottle filled with water nearby in case plank begins to burn. If it flares up, spray lightly with water.

**6.** Lightly brush grid with oil and place soaked plank on top. Cover, heat until plank smokes and crackles. Place salmon, skin side down, on plank and arrange mango skewers alongside plank. Cover. Grill 6 to 8 minutes, turning skewers frequently, until mango pieces are slightly charred. Remove mango from the grill; set aside. Cover; grill salmon 9 to 12 minutes or until the flesh begins to flake when tested with fork.

**7.** Remove plank from grill and transfer salmon to serving platter. Slide mango pieces off skewers and add to mint mixture, tossing gently to coat. Serve immediately alongside salmon.

**tip:** Cedar planks can be purchased at gourmet kitchen stores or hardware stores. Be sure to buy untreated wood at least ½ inch thick. Use each plank for grilling food only once. Used planks may be broken up into wood chips and used to smoke foods.

# fukien red-cooked pork

MAKES 4 TO 5 SERVINGS

5¼ cups plus 3 tablespoons water, divided

2 pounds boneless pork shoulder, well trimmed, cut into 1½-inch chunks

⅓ cup rice wine or dry sherry

⅓ cup reduced-sodium soy sauce

2 tablespoons lightly packed light brown sugar

1 piece fresh ginger (about 1½ inches), peeled and cut into strips

3 cloves garlic, chopped

1 teaspoon anise seeds

2 tablespoons cornstarch

1 pound carrots, diagonally sliced

½ head napa cabbage (about 1 pound), core removed, cut into 1-inch slices

1 teaspoon sesame oil

**1.** Place 4 cups water in wok; bring to a boil over high heat. Add pork chunks; return to a boil. Boil pork 2 minutes. Drain in colander; return pork to wok. Add 1¼ cups water, wine, soy sauce, brown sugar, ginger, garlic and anise. Cover; bring mixture to a boil. Reduce heat to low and simmer 1¼ hours or until meat is almost tender, stirring occasionally.

**2.** Stir remaining 3 tablespoons water and cornstarch in cup until smooth; set aside.

**3.** Add carrots to wok; cover and cook 20 minutes or until pork and carrots are fork-tender. Transfer with slotted spoon to serving bowl.

**4.** Add cabbage to liquid in wok. Cover and increase heat to medium-high. Cook cabbage about 2 minutes or until wilted. Stir cornstarch mixture until smooth; add to cabbage. Cook until sauce boils and thickens. Return pork and carrots to wok; add oil and mix well. Spoon mixture into serving bowl.

**note:** "Red cooking" is a Chinese cooking method in which meat or poultry is braised in soy sauce, giving the meat a deep, rich color.

# grilled tilapia with zesty mustard sauce

MAKES 4 SERVINGS

1 tablespoon olive oil

1 teaspoon Dijon mustard

½ teaspoon grated lemon peel

½ teaspoon Worcestershire sauce (lowest sodium available)

½ teaspoon salt, divided

¼ teaspoon black pepper

4 mild thin fish fillets, such as tilapia (about 4 ounces each)

1½ teaspoons paprika

½ medium lemon, quartered

2 tablespoons minced fresh parsley (optional)

**1.** Prepare grill for direct cooking over high heat.

**2.** Stir together oil, mustard, lemon peel, Worcestershire sauce, ¼ teaspoon salt and pepper in small bowl until well blended. Set aside.

**3.** Rinse fish and pat dry with paper towels. Sprinkle both sides of fish with paprika and remaining ¼ teaspoon salt. Lightly spray grill basket with nonstick cooking spray. Place fish in the basket. Grill, covered, 3 minutes. Turn and grill, covered, 2 to 3 minutes, or until fish flakes easily when tested with fork. Transfer to platter.

**4.** Squeeze 1 lemon wedge over each fillet. Spread mustard mixture evenly over fish; garnish with parsley.

# broiled turkey tenderloin kabobs

MAKES 4 SERVINGS

¼ cup orange juice

2 tablespoons reduced-sodium soy sauce, divided

1 clove garlic, minced

1 teaspoon fresh grated ginger

12 ounces turkey tenderloin (about 2 medium), cut into 1-inch cubes

1 tablespoon molasses

1 green bell pepper, cut into 1-inch pieces

1 red onion, cut into 1½-inch pieces

1 cup hot cooked brown rice

**1.** Combine orange juice, 1 tablespoon soy sauce, garlic and ginger in large bowl; measure out half of mixture; cover and refrigerate. Add turkey to remaining mixture. Cover and marinate 2 hours, stirring occasionally.

**2.** Line baking sheet with foil; spray with nonstick cooking spray. Remove turkey from marinade; discard marinade. Add remaining 1 tablespoon soy sauce and molasses to reserved half of marinade; whisk until smooth and well blended.

**3.** Alternately thread turkey, bell pepper and onion on 4 skewers.* Place on prepared baking sheet.

**4.** Broil 4 inches from heat source 3 minutes. Brush evenly with reserved marinade mixture. Broil 6 to 9 minutes or until turkey is no longer pink.

**5.** Spoon ¼ cup brown rice onto 4 plates. Top each with 1 skewer.

*If using wooden skewers, soak in cold water 20 to 30 minutes to prevent burning.*

# pan-seared sole with lemon-butter caper sauce

MAKES 2 SERVINGS

¼ cup whole wheat flour
½ teaspoon salt
¼ teaspoon black pepper
1 pound Dover sole fillets
2 tablespoons olive oil
2 tablespoons lemon juice
2 teaspoons capers, rinsed, drained and chopped
2 tablespoons finely chopped fresh chives

**1.** Combine flour, salt and pepper in shallow dish or pie plate. Coat fillets with flour mixture, shaking off excess.

**2.** Heat oil in large nonstick skillet over medium heat. Add half of fillets; cook 2 to 3 minutes per side or until golden brown. Transfer to plate and tent with foil to keep warm. Repeat with remaining fillets.

**3.** Stir lemon juice and capers in small bowl.

**4.** Drizzle lemon juice mixture over fish; sprinkle with chives. Serve immediately.

# chicken and spinach salad

MAKES 4 SERVINGS

¾ pound chicken tenders

4 cups shredded stemmed spinach

2 cups washed and torn romaine lettuce

1 large grapefruit, peeled and sectioned

8 thin slices red onion, separated into rings

2 tablespoons crumbled reduced-fat blue cheese

½ cup frozen citrus blend concentrate, thawed

¼ cup prepared fat-free Italian salad dressing

**1.** Cut chicken into 2×½-inch strips. Spray large nonstick skillet with nonstick cooking spray; heat over medium heat. Add chicken; cook and stir 5 minutes or until no longer pink in center. Remove from skillet.

**2.** Divide spinach, lettuce, grapefruit, onion, cheese and chicken among 4 salad plates. Combine citrus blend concentrate and Italian dressing in small bowl; drizzle over salads.

# roast dill scrod with asparagus

MAKES 4 SERVINGS

1 bunch (12 ounces) asparagus spears, ends trimmed

1 teaspoon olive oil

4 scrod or cod fillets (about 5 ounces each)

1 tablespoon lemon juice

1 teaspoon dried dill weed

½ teaspoon salt

¼ teaspoon black pepper

Paprika (optional)

**1.** Preheat oven to 425°F.

**2.** Place asparagus in 13×9-inch baking dish; drizzle with oil. Roll asparagus to coat lightly with oil; push to edges of dish, stacking asparagus into 2 layers.

**3.** Arrange fish fillets in center of dish; drizzle with lemon juice. Combine dill, salt and pepper in small bowl; sprinkle over fish and asparagus. Sprinkle with paprika, if desired.

**4.** Roast 15 to 17 minutes or until asparagus is crisp-tender and fish is opaque in center and begins to flake when tested with fork.

# pork tenderloin with cabbage

MAKES 6 SERVINGS

¼ cup chicken broth or water

3 cups shredded red cabbage

¼ cup chopped onion

1 clove garlic, minced

1½ pounds pork tenderloin

¾ cup apple juice concentrate

3 tablespoons honey mustard

1½ tablespoons Worcestershire sauce

**1.** Preheat oven to 450°F. Pour broth into shallow nonstick roasting pan; heat on stovetop over medium heat. Add cabbage, onion and garlic; cook and stir 2 to 3 minutes or until cabbage wilts.

**2.** Add pork to roasting pan. (If using 2 small tenderloins, place side-by-side.) Transfer pan to oven; roast 10 minutes.

**3.** Meanwhile, combine apple juice concentrate, mustard and Worcestershire sauce in small bowl. Pour half of mixture over pork. Roast 10 minutes.

**4.** Baste pork with half of remaining apple juice mixture; stir remaining half into cabbage. Roast 15 to 20 minutes or until meat thermometer inserted in center of pork registers 160°F. Let stand 5 minutes. Slice pork and serve with cabbage and pan juices.

# kale & mushroom
# stuffed chicken breasts

MAKES 4 SERVINGS

3 teaspoons olive oil, divided

1 cup coarsely chopped mushrooms

2 cups thinly sliced kale

1 tablespoon fresh lemon juice

½ teaspoon salt, divided

4 boneless skinless chicken breasts (about 4 ounces each)

¼ cup crumbled reduced-fat feta cheese

¼ teaspoon black pepper

**1.** Heat 1 teaspoon oil in large skillet over medium-high heat. Add mushrooms; cook and stir 5 minutes or until mushrooms begin to brown. Add kale; cook and stir 8 minutes or until wilted. Sprinkle with lemon juice and ¼ teaspoon salt. Remove to small bowl. Let stand 5 to 10 minutes to cool slightly.

**2.** Meanwhile, place each chicken breast between sheets of plastic wrap. Pound with meat mallet or rolling pin to about ½-inch thickness.

**3.** Gently stir feta cheese into mushroom and kale mixture. Spoon ¼ cup mixture down center of each chicken breast. Roll up to enclose filling; secure with toothpicks. Sprinkle with remaining ¼ teaspoon salt and pepper.

**4.** Wipe out same skillet with paper towels. Add remaining 2 teaspoons oil to skillet; heat over medium heat. Add chicken; brown on all sides. Cover and cook 5 minutes per side or until no longer pink. Remove toothpicks before serving.

**serving suggestion:** Serve this flavorful entrée with a fresh salad or summer vegetables.

# salmon salad with basil vinaigrette

## MAKES 4 SERVINGS

Basil Vinaigrette (recipe follows)

1¼ teaspoons salt, divided

1 pound asparagus, trimmed

1 pound salmon fillet

1½ teaspoons olive oil

¼ teaspoon black pepper

4 lemon wedges

**1.** Prepare Basil Vinaigrette. Preheat oven to 400°F or prepare grill for direct cooking over medium-high heat.

**2.** Combine 3 inches water and 1 teaspoon salt in large saucepan; bring to boil over high heat. Add asparagus; simmer 6 to 8 minutes or until crisp-tender; drain and set aside.

**3.** Brush salmon with oil. Sprinkle with remaining ¼ teaspoon salt and pepper. Place fish in shallow baking pan; cook 11 to 13 minutes or until center is opaque. (Or, grill on well-oiled grid over medium-high heat 4 or 5 minutes per side or until center is opaque.)

**4.** Remove skin from salmon; break into bite-size pieces. Arrange salmon over asparagus; drizzle with Basil Vinaigrette. Serve with lemon wedges.

## basil vinaigrette

### MAKES ABOUT ¼ CUP

3 tablespoons olive oil

1 tablespoon white wine vinegar

1 tablespoon minced fresh basil

1 clove garlic, minced

1 teaspoon minced fresh chives

¼ teaspoon black pepper

⅛ teaspoon salt

Combine all ingredients in small bowl; stir until blended.

# roast sesame fish

## MAKES 4 SERVINGS

4   skinless tilapia fillets (about 5 ounces each)

¼   cup plus 1 tablespoon reduced-sodium tamari or soy sauce, divided

1   teaspoon dark sesame oil, divided

2   teaspoons sesame seeds

2   tablespoons sake or dry sherry

2   to 3 teaspoons grated fresh ginger

1   teaspoon sugar

1   teaspoon wasabi paste (optional)

**1.** Preheat oven to 400°F. Place fish in shallow baking dish. Combine 1 tablespoon tamari and ½ teaspoon sesame oil in small bowl; brush over fish. Sprinkle sesame seeds over fish. Bake 10 to 15 minutes or until fish is opaque in center.

**2.** Meanwhile, combine remaining ¼ cup tamari, ½ teaspoon sesame oil, sake, ginger, sugar and wasabi paste, if desired, in small bowl. Drizzle sauce over fish before serving.

# asian pesto noodles

Spicy Asian Pesto
(recipe follows)

1  pound large raw shrimp,
   peeled and deveined

12  ounces uncooked soba
    (buckwheat) noodles

**1.** Prepare Spicy Asian Pesto. Marinate shrimp in ¾ cup pesto.

**2.** Cook soba noodles according to package directions; drain and set aside. Preheat broiler or grill.

**3.** Place marinated shrimp on metal skewers. (If using wooden skewers, soak in water for at least 30 minutes to prevent burning.) Place skewers under broiler or on grill; cook about 3 minutes per side or until shrimp are opaque.

**4.** To serve, toss soba noodles with remaining pesto. Serve with shrimp.

## spicy asian pesto

MAKES 2½ CUPS

3  cups fresh basil

3  cups fresh cilantro

3  cups fresh mint

¾  cup peanut oil

1  tablespoon sugar

2  to 3 tablespoons lime juice

5  cloves garlic, chopped

2  teaspoons fish sauce *or*
   1 teaspoon salt

1  serrano pepper,* finely
   chopped

*Serrano peppers can sting and irritate the skin, so wear rubber gloves when handling peppers and do not touch your eyes.*

Combine all ingredients in blender or food processor; blend until smooth.

# sizzling rice flour crêpes

MAKES 4 TO 6 SERVINGS

## crêpes

- 1 cup rice flour
- ½ teaspoon salt
- ½ teaspoon sugar
- ½ teaspoon ground turmeric
- 1 cup unsweetened coconut milk
- ½ to ¾ cup water
- ½ cup vegetable oil

## filling

- 1 bunch green onions, chopped
- 1 cup chopped cooked chicken *or* 1 cup small raw shrimp, peeled *or* 1 cup cubed tofu
- 2 cups bean sprouts
  Lettuce, fresh cilantro and fresh mint

## dipping sauce

- ⅔ cup water
- ¼ cup gluten-free fish sauce
- 1 tablespoon sugar
  Juice of 1 lime
- 1 clove garlic, minced
- 1 serrano or other hot pepper, minced
- 1 to 2 tablespoons shredded carrot

**1.** Combine rice flour salt, sugar and turmeric in medium bowl. Gradually whisk in coconut milk and ½ cup water until batter is thickness of heavy cream. Let batter rest at least 10 minutes. Add additional water as needed to thin batter.

**2.** Heat 9- or 10-inch nonstick skillet over medium heat. Add 3 teaspoons oil to skillet. Add choice of ¼ cup filling to skillet (about 1 tablespoon green onion, plus 3 tablespoons chicken, shrimp, tofu or a combination). Cook and stir 2 to 4 minutes or until onions are softened and shrimp is pink and opaque, if using. Pour about ½ cup batter over filling mixture. Immediately swirl to coat bottom of pan with batter; allow some batter to go up side of pan.

**3.** In 30 seconds or when sizzling sound stops, add bean sprouts to 1 side of crêpe. Cover pan and cook 3 minutes or until sprouts wilt and center of crêpe appears cooked. Edges should be browned and crisp.

**4.** Fold crêpe in half with spatula and transfer to plate. Repeat with remaining batter and fillings.

**5.** For dipping sauce, combine ⅔ cup water, fish sauce, sugar and lime juice in small bowl. Stir until sugar dissolves. Stir in garlic and pepper; top with carrot.

**6.** Serve crêpes with Dipping Sauce.

# meatless
# MEALS

## quinoa with tomato, broccoli and feta

MAKES 4 SERVINGS

⅔ cup uncooked quinoa

1½ cups small broccoli florets

1 plum tomato, diced

⅓ cup (1½ ounces) crumbled reduced-fat feta cheese

2 tablespoons lemon juice

1 tablespoon extra virgin olive oil

¼ teaspoon dried dill weed *or* dried basil

¼ teaspoon kosher salt (optional)

⅛ teaspoon black pepper

**1.** Cook quinoa according to package directions omitting any salt or fat. Transfer to large bowl; cool to lukewarm.

**2.** Steam broccoli in steamer basket over boiling water 3 minutes or until just tender.

**3.** Combine quinoa, broccoli, tomato and feta cheese in medium bowl.

**4.** Whisk lemon juice, oil, dill weed, salt, if desired, and pepper in small bowl. Pour over salad; toss gently.

# soba stir-fry

MAKES 4 SERVINGS

8 ounces uncooked soba (buckwheat) noodles

1 tablespoon olive oil

2 cups sliced shiitake mushrooms

1 medium red bell pepper, cut into thin strips

2 whole dried red chiles *or* ¼ teaspoon red pepper flakes

1 clove garlic, minced

2 cups shredded napa cabbage

½ cup fat-free reduced-sodium vegetable broth

2 tablespoons reduced-sodium tamari or soy sauce

1 tablespoon rice wine or dry sherry

2 teaspoons cornstarch

1 package (14 ounces) firm tofu, drained and cut into 1-inch cubes

2 green onions, thinly sliced

**1.** Cook noodles according to package directions, omitting salt. Drain and set aside.

**2.** Heat oil in large nonstick skillet or wok over medium-high heat. Add mushrooms, bell pepper, dried chiles and garlic. Cook and stir 3 minutes or until mushrooms are tender. Add cabbage. Cover; cook 2 minutes or until cabbage is wilted.

**3.** Whisk broth, tamari and rice wine into cornstarch in small bowl until smooth. Stir sauce into vegetable mixture. Cook 2 minutes or until sauce is thickened.

**4.** Stir tofu and noodles into vegetable mixture; toss gently until heated through. Sprinkle with green onions. Serve immediately.

# brown rice & vegetable stuffed squash

MAKES 4 SERVINGS

2 large acorn or golden acorn squash (about 1½ pounds each)

1 cup uncooked quick-cooking brown rice

2 cups broccoli florets, chopped

½ teaspoon salt

½ teaspoon black pepper

¼ cup chopped almonds,* toasted

¾ cup (3 ounces) shredded reduced-fat Cheddar cheese

*To toast almonds, spread in single layer in heavy skillet. Cook and stir over medium heat 1 to 2 minutes or until nuts are lightly browned, stirring frequently.*

**1.** Preheat oven to 375°F. Cut squash in half crosswise; scrape out and discard seeds. Trim off stems and a small portion of pointed ends to allow squash to stand when turned over. Place squash halves cut side down on microwavable plate; microwave on HIGH 12 to 15 minutes, or until almost tender when pierced. Place squash halves in 13×9-inch baking pan, cut side up. Cover; let stand 3 minutes or until ready to fill.

**2.** Meanwhile, cook rice according to package directions, adding broccoli, salt and pepper during last 5 minutes of cooking. Stir in almonds.

**3.** Mound rice mixture into squash, overflowing into dish if necessary; sprinkle with cheese. Bake 20 to 25 minutes or until squash is tender and cheese is melted.

# scrambled tofu and potatoes

MAKES 4 SERVINGS

## potatoes

¼ cup olive oil

4 red potatoes, cubed

½ white onion, sliced

1 tablespoon chopped fresh rosemary

½ teaspoon coarse salt

## scrambled tofu

¼ cup nutritional yeast

½ teaspoon ground turmeric

2 tablespoons water

2 tablespoons reduced-sodium soy sauce

1 package (14 ounces) firm tofu

2 teaspoons olive oil

½ cup chopped green bell pepper

½ cup chopped red onion

**1.** For potatoes, preheat oven to 450°F. Add ¼ cup oil to 12-inch cast-iron skillet; place skillet in oven 10 minutes to heat.

**2.** Bring large saucepan of water to a boil. Add potatoes; cook 5 to 7 minutes or until tender. Drain and return to saucepan; stir in white onion, rosemary and salt. Spread mixture in preheated skillet. Bake 25 to 30 minutes or until potatoes are browned, stirring every 10 minutes.

**3.** For tofu, combine nutritional yeast and turmeric in small bowl. Stir in water and soy sauce until smooth.

**4.** Cut tofu into large cubes. Gently squeeze out water; loosely crumble tofu into medium bowl. Heat 2 teaspoons oil in large skillet over medium-high heat. Add bell pepper and red onion; cook and stir 2 minutes or until soft but not browned. Add tofu; drizzle with 3 tablespoons nutritional yeast sauce. Cook and stir about 5 minutes or until liquid is evaporated and tofu is heated through. Stir in additional sauce for stronger flavor, if desired.

**5.** Divide potatoes among 4 serving plates; top with tofu mixture.

# quinoa-stuffed eggplant

MAKES 2 SERVINGS

1   eggplant
¼   cup uncooked quinoa
½   cup water
2   teaspoons olive oil
½   cup chopped onion
1   clove garlic, chopped
2   cups baby spinach, finely
    chopped
¼   cup crumbled reduced-fat
    feta cheese, divided
    Juice of 1 lemon
    Chopped fresh parsley
    (optional)

**1.** Preheat oven to 400°F. Slice eggplant in half lengthwise. Scoop out flesh, leaving ½-inch shell. Finely chop scooped out flesh and set aside. Place eggplant halves in baking dish. Bake 30 minutes. *Reduce oven temperature to 350°F.*

**2.** Meanwhile, place quinoa in fine-mesh strainer; rinse well under cold running water. Bring water to a boil in small saucepan; stir in quinoa. Reduce heat to low; cover and simmer 10 to 15 minutes or until quinoa is tender and water is absorbed.

**3.** Heat oil in large skillet over medium-high heat. Add onion and chopped eggplant; cook and stir 10 minutes or until vegetables are browned and tender. Add garlic; cook and stir 1 minute. Remove from heat. Stir in quinoa, spinach, 2 tablespoons feta cheese and lemon juice.

**4.** Spoon quinoa mixture evenly into eggplant shells. Top evenly with remaining 2 tablespoons feta cheese.

**5.** Bake 15 minutes or until eggplant has softened and cheese is browned. Garnish with parsley.

# spicy sesame noodles

## MAKES 6 SERVINGS

6 ounces uncooked soba (buckwheat) noodles

2 teaspoons dark sesame oil

1 tablespoon sesame seeds

½ cup fat-free reduced-sodium vegetable broth

1 tablespoon creamy peanut butter

½ cup thinly sliced green onions

½ cup minced red bell pepper

4 teaspoons reduced-sodium soy sauce

1½ teaspoons finely chopped seeded jalapeño pepper*

1 clove garlic, minced

¼ teaspoon red pepper flakes

*Jalapeño peppers can sting and irritate the skin, so wear rubber gloves when handling peppers and do not touch your eyes.

**1.** Cook noodles according to package directions. (Do not overcook.) Rinse noodles thoroughly with cold running water; drain. Place noodles in large bowl; toss with oil.

**2.** Cook sesame seeds in small skillet over medium heat about 3 minutes or until seeds begin to pop and turn golden brown, stirring frequently. Remove from skillet.

**3.** Whisk broth and peanut butter in medium bowl until blended. (Mixture may look curdled.) Stir in green onions, bell pepper, soy sauce, jalapeño pepper, garlic and red pepper flakes.

**4.** Pour mixture over noodles; toss to coat. Cover and let stand 30 minutes at room temperature or refrigerate up to 24 hours. Sprinkle with toasted sesame seeds before serving.

# vegetarian quinoa chili

## MAKES 4 TO 6 SERVINGS

2 tablespoons olive oil

1 large onion

1 red bell pepper, diced

1 large carrot, peeled and diced

1 stalk celery, diced

1 jalapeño pepper,* seeded and finely chopped

1 tablespoon minced garlic

3 tablespoons chili powder

2 teaspoons ground cumin

1 teaspoon kosher salt

1 can (about 15 ounces) kidney beans, rinsed and drained

1 can (28 ounces) crushed tomatoes

1 cup water

1 cup fresh or frozen corn

½ cup uncooked quinoa, rinsed well

Diced avocado, shredded reduced-fat Cheddar cheese and sliced green onions (optional)

*Jalapeño peppers can sting and irritate the skin, so wear rubber gloves when handling peppers and do not touch your eyes.*

**1.** Heat oil over medium-high heat in large saucepan. Add onion, bell pepper, carrot and celery; cook about 10 minutes until softened, stirring occasionally. Add jalapeño pepper, garlic, chili powder, cumin and salt; cook about 1 minute or until fragrant.

**2.** Add beans, tomatoes, water, corn and quinoa; bring to a boil. Reduce heat to low; cover and simmer 1 hour, stirring occasionally.

**3.** Spoon into bowls; garnish with toppings as desired.

# zucchini and sweet potato stuffed peppers

MAKES 4 SERVINGS

4   red bell peppers (about 6 ounces each)

2   teaspoons olive oil

1   medium zucchini (8 ounces), thinly sliced

1   small onion, thinly sliced

½   cup diced celery

1   teaspoon Italian seasoning

½   teaspoon salt (optional)

¼   teaspoon black pepper

1   sweet potato, peeled and finely diced

¼   cup vegetable broth

2   tablespoons toasted pine nuts*

*To toast pine nuts, spread in single layer in heavy skillet. Cook over medium heat 1 to 2 minutes or until nuts are lightly browned, stirring frequently.*

**1.** Preheat oven to 375°F. Spray baking dish with nonstick cooking spray.

**2.** Slice tops off bell peppers; remove seeds and membranes. Bring large pot of water to a boil. Add bell peppers; cover and cook 5 minutes or until bell peppers start to soften. Remove with tongs; drain upside down.

**3.** Heat oil in large skillet over medium-high heat. Add zucchini, onion, celery, Italian seasoning, salt, if desired, and black pepper; cook 5 to 7 minutes or until zucchini is browned and vegetables are tender, stirring occasionally. Add sweet potato during last 3 minutes of cooking. Reduce heat if browning too quickly.

**4.** Combine zucchini mixture, broth and pine nuts in large bowl; spoon into bell peppers. Transfer to prepared baking dish. Bake 15 minutes or until sweet potato is tender and filling is heated through.

# roasted vegetable salad
# with capers and walnuts

1 pound small Brussels sprouts, trimmed

1 pound unpeeled small Yukon Gold potatoes, cut into halves

¼ teaspoon salt

¼ teaspoon black pepper

¼ teaspoon dried rosemary

5 tablespoons olive oil, divided

1 red bell pepper, cut into bite-size pieces

¼ cup walnuts, coarsely chopped

2 tablespoons capers, drained

1½ tablespoons white wine vinegar

**1.** Preheat oven to 400°F.

**2.** Slash bottoms of Brussels sprouts; place in shallow roasting pan. Add potatoes; sprinkle with salt, black pepper and rosemary. Drizzle with 3 tablespoons oil; toss to coat. Roast 20 minutes. Stir in bell pepper; roast 15 minutes or until tender. Transfer to large bowl; stir in walnuts and capers.

**3.** Whisk remaining 2 tablespoons oil and vinegar in small bowl until blended. Pour over salad; toss to coat. Serve at room temperature.

# buckwheat with zucchini and mushrooms

## MAKES 6 SERVINGS

1½ to 2 tablespoons olive oil

1 cup sliced mushrooms

1 medium zucchini, cut into ½-inch pieces

1 medium onion, chopped

1 clove garlic, minced

¾ cup buckwheat

¼ teaspoon dried thyme

¼ teaspoon salt

⅛ teaspoon black pepper

1¼ cups vegetable broth

Lemon wedges (optional)

**1.** Heat oil in large nonstick skillet over medium heat. Add mushrooms, zucchini, onion and garlic. Cook and stir 7 to 10 minutes or until vegetables are tender. Add buckwheat, thyme, salt and pepper; cook and stir 2 minutes.

**2.** Add broth; bring to a boil. Cover; reduce heat to low. Cook 10 to 13 minutes or until liquid is absorbed and buckwheat is tender. Remove from heat; let stand, covered, 5 minutes. Serve with lemon wedges, if desired.

# vegetarian paella

MAKES 6 SERVINGS

2 teaspoons olive oil

1 cup chopped onion

2 cloves garlic, minced

1 cup uncooked brown rice

2¼ cups vegetable broth

1 teaspoon Italian seasoning

¾ teaspoon salt (optional)

½ teaspoon ground turmeric

⅛ teaspoon ground red pepper

1 can (about 14 ounces) no-salt-added stewed tomatoes

1 cup chopped red bell pepper

1 cup coarsely chopped carrots

1 can (14 ounces) quartered artichoke hearts, drained

1 small zucchini, halved lengthwise and sliced to ¼-inch thickness (about 1¼ cups)

½ cup frozen baby peas

**1.** Heat oil in large nonstick skillet over medium-high heat. Add onion and garlic; cook 6 to 7 minutes or until onion is translucent. Reduce heat to medium-low. Stir in rice; cook and stir 1 minute.

**2.** Add broth, Italian seasoning, salt, if desired, turmeric and ground red pepper. Bring to a boil. Cover and simmer 30 minutes.

**3.** Stir in tomatoes, bell pepper and carrots. Cover and simmer 10 minutes.

**4.** Reduce heat to low. Stir in artichoke hearts, zucchini and peas. Cover and cook 10 minutes or until vegetables are crisp-tender.

# sides &
# SALADS

## nutty vegetable duo
### MAKES 4 SERVINGS

1 package (10 ounces) frozen green beans

½ package (16 ounces) frozen small whole onions

¼ cup toasted slivered almonds*

Salt and black pepper

*To toast almonds, spread in single layer in heavy skillet. Cook and stir over medium heat 1 to 2 minutes or until nuts are lightly browned, stirring frequently.*

**1.** Combine beans and onions in medium saucepan; cook according to package directions. Drain.

**2.** Return vegetables to saucepan. Add almonds; stir over low heat until mixture is thoroughly heated. Season with salt and pepper.

# apple stuffed acorn squash

MAKES 8 SERVINGS

¼ cup raisins

2 acorn squash (about 4 inches in diameter)

1 tablespoon sugar

¼ teaspoon ground cinnamon

2 medium Fuji apples, cut into ½-inch pieces

**1.** Cover raisins with warm water and soak 20 minutes. Preheat oven to 375°F.

**2.** Cut squash into quarters; remove seeds. Place squash on baking sheet. Combine sugar and cinnamon in small bowl; sprinkle half of cinnamon mixture over squash. Bake 10 minutes.

**3.** Meanwhile, drain raisins. Combine raisins, apples and remaining cinnamon mixture in medium bowl. Top partially baked squash with apple mixture. Bake 30 to 35 minutes or until apples and squash are tender. Serve warm.

# veggie-quinoa and brown rice pilaf

## MAKES 6 SERVINGS

2 cups water

1 cup instant brown rice

½ cup uncooked quinoa, preferably the tri-colored variety

½ cup pine nuts *or* slivered almonds

2 tablespoons olive oil, divided

1 cup chopped onions

1 package (8 ounces) sliced baby Portobello mushrooms

1 clove garlic, minced

½ cup finely chopped red bell pepper *or* seeded diced tomato

1 teaspoon chopped fresh rosemary

¾ teaspoon salt

Black pepper

¼ cup crumbled reduced-fat blue cheese (optional)

**1.** Heat water to a boil in medium saucepan over high heat. Stir in rice and quinoa, return to a boil, reduce heat to low. Cover; simmer 12 minutes or until water is absorbed.

**2.** Meanwhile, heat large skillet over medium-high heat. Add pine nuts; cook 1½ to 2 minutes or until beginning to brown, stirring constantly. Set aside on separate plate.

**3.** Heat 1 tablespoon oil in large skillet over medium-high heat. Add onions; cook 6 minutes or until beginning to richly brown. Stir in mushrooms; cook 5 to 6 minutes or until beginning to brown on edges. Stir in garlic; cook 15 seconds, stirring constantly. Remove from heat.

**4.** Stir in remaining 1 tablespoon oil, bell pepper, rosemary, salt, rice-quinoa mixture and pine nuts. Season with black pepper. Sprinkle with cheese, if desired.

# sweet & savory sweet potato salad

MAKES 6 SERVINGS

4 cups peeled chopped cooked sweet potatoes (about 4 to 6)

¾ cup chopped green onions

½ cup chopped fresh parsley

½ cup dried unsweetened cherries

¼ cup plus 2 tablespoons rice wine vinegar

2 tablespoons coarse ground mustard

1 tablespoon extra virgin olive oil

¾ teaspoon garlic powder

¼ teaspoon black pepper

⅛ teaspoon salt

**1.** Combine sweet potatoes, green onions, parsley and cherries in large bowl; gently mix.

**2.** Whisk vinegar, mustard, oil, garlic powder, pepper and salt in small bowl until well blended. Pour over sweet potato mixture; gently toss to coat. Serve immediately or cover and refrigerate until ready to serve.

# roasted sweet potato and apple salad

MAKES 4 SERVINGS

2 large sweet potatoes, peeled and cubed

½ teaspoon salt, divided

¼ teaspoon black pepper

3 tablespoons low-calorie apple juice cocktail

1 tablespoon olive oil

1 tablespoon balsamic vinegar

1 tablespoon Dijon mustard

1 tablespoon honey

2 teaspoons snipped fresh chives

1 medium Gala apple, diced (about 1 cup)

½ cup finely chopped celery

¼ cup thinly sliced red onion

Lettuce leaves

**1.** Preheat oven to 450°F. Arrange sweet potatoes in single layer on baking sheet. Spray with nonstick cooking spray; season with ¼ teaspoon salt and pepper.

**2.** Roast 20 to 25 minutes or until potatoes are tender, stirring halfway through cooking time. Cool completely.

**3.** Meanwhile, whisk apple juice cocktail, oil, vinegar, mustard, honey, chives and remaining ¼ teaspoon salt in small bowl until smooth and well blended.

**4.** Combine sweet potatoes, apple, celery and onion in medium bowl. Drizzle with dressing; gently toss to coat. Arrange lettuce leaves on 4 serving plates. Top evenly with sweet potato mixture.

# mediterranean vegetable bake

## MAKES 4 TO 6 SERVINGS

2 tomatoes, sliced

1 small red onion, sliced

1 medium zucchini, sliced

1 small eggplant, sliced

1 small yellow squash, sliced

1 large portobello mushroom, sliced

2 cloves garlic, finely chopped

3 tablespoons olive oil

2 teaspoons chopped fresh rosemary leaves

⅔ cup dry white wine

Salt and black pepper

**1.** Preheat oven to 350°F. Grease bottom of oval casserole or 13×9-inch baking dish.

**2.** Arrange slices of vegetables in rows, alternating different types and overlapping slices in pan to make attractive arrangement; sprinkle evenly with garlic. Combine oil and rosemary in small bowl; drizzle over vegetables.

**3.** Pour wine over vegetables; season with salt and pepper. Cover loosely with foil. Bake 20 minutes. Uncover; bake 10 to 15 minutes or until vegetables are tender.

# light lemon cauliflower

## MAKES 6 SERVINGS

4 tablespoons chopped fresh parsley, divided

½ teaspoon grated lemon peel

6 cups (about 1½ pounds) cauliflower florets

1 tablespoon olive oil

3 cloves garlic, minced

2 tablespoons fresh lemon juice

¼ cup grated Parmesan cheese (optional)

Lemon slices (optional)

**1.** Place 1 tablespoon parsley, lemon peel and about 1 inch water in large saucepan. Place cauliflower in steamer basket; place in saucepan. Bring water to a boil over medium heat. Cover; steam 14 to 16 minutes or until cauliflower is crisp-tender. Remove to large bowl; keep warm. Reserve ½ cup hot liquid.

**2.** Heat oil in small saucepan over medium heat. Add garlic; cook and stir 2 to 3 minutes or until soft. Stir in lemon juice and reserved liquid.

**3.** Spoon lemon sauce over cauliflower. Sprinkle with remaining 3 tablespoons parsley and cheese, if desired, before serving. Garnish with lemon slices.

# spinach salad with pomegranate vinaigrette

## MAKES 4 SERVINGS

- 1 package (5 ounces) baby spinach
- ½ cup pomegranate seeds (arils)
- ¼ cup crumbled reduced-fat goat cheese
- 2 tablespoons chopped walnuts, toasted*
- ¼ cup pomegranate juice
- 2 tablespoons olive oil
- 1 tablespoon red wine vinegar
- 1 tablespoon honey
- ¼ teaspoon salt
- ¼ teaspoon black pepper

*To toast walnuts, spread in single layer in heavy-bottomed skillet. Cook over medium heat 1 to 2 minutes until nuts are lightly browned, stirring frequently. Remove from skillet immediately. Cool before using.*

**1.** Combine spinach, pomegranate seeds, goat cheese and walnuts in large bowl.

**2.** Whisk pomegranate juice, oil, vinegar, honey, salt and pepper in small bowl until well blended. Pour over salad; gently toss to coat. Serve immediately.

**tip:** For easier removal of pomegranate seeds, cut a pomegranate into pieces and immerse in a bowl of cold water. The membrane that holds the seeds in place will float to the top; discard it and collect the seeds. For convenience, you can find containers of ready-to-use pomegranate seeds in the refrigerated produce section of some supermarkets.

# marinated vegetables

¼ cup rice wine vinegar

3 tablespoons reduced-sodium soy sauce

2 tablespoons fresh lemon juice

1 tablespoon vegetable oil

1 clove garlic, minced

1 teaspoon minced fresh ginger

½ teaspoon sugar

2 cups broccoli florets

2 cups cauliflower florets

2 cups diagonally sliced carrots (½-inch pieces)

8 ounces whole fresh mushrooms

1 large red bell pepper, cut into 1-inch pieces

Lettuce leaves

**1.** Combine vinegar, soy sauce, lemon juice, oil, garlic, ginger and sugar in large bowl. Set aside.

**2.** To blanch broccoli, cauliflower and carrots, cook 1 minute in enough salted boiling water to cover. Remove and plunge into cold water, then drain immediately. Add to oil mixture in bowl while still warm; toss to coat. Cool to room temperature.

**3.** Add mushrooms and bell pepper to vegetables in bowl; toss to coat. Cover and marinate in refrigerator at least 4 hours or up to 24 hours. Drain vegetables, reserving marinade.

**4.** Arrange vegetables on lettuce-lined platter. Serve chilled or at room temperature with toothpicks. Serve remaining marinade in small cup for dipping, if desired.

# spicy grapefruit salad with raspberry dressing

2 cups washed watercress

2 cups mixed salad greens

3 medium grapefruit, peeled, sectioned and seeded

½ pound jicama, cut into thin strips

1 cup fresh raspberries

2 tablespoons chopped green onion

1 tablespoon honey

1 teaspoon balsamic vinegar

½ to ¾ teaspoon dry mustard

**1.** Combine watercress and salad greens in large bowl; divide evenly among 4 plates. Top evenly with grapefruit and jicama.

**2.** Reserve 12 raspberries for garnish. Combine remaining raspberries, green onion, honey, vinegar and mustard in food processor or blender; process until smooth and well blended.

**3.** Drizzle dressing over salads. Top each salad with 3 reserved raspberries. Serve immediately.

132 sides & salads

# cabbage and red potato salad
# with cilantro-lime dressing

½ cup finely chopped fresh cilantro

2 tablespoons fresh lime juice

2 tablespoons olive oil

2 teaspoons honey

½ teaspoon ground cumin

¼ teaspoon salt

2 cups sliced napa cabbage

2 cups sliced red cabbage

¾ pound baby red potatoes (about 4 potatoes), quartered and cooked

½ cup sliced green onions

2 tablespoons unsalted sunflower kernels

**1.** Whisk cilantro, lime juice, oil, honey, cumin and salt in small bowl until smooth and well blended. Let stand 30 minutes to allow flavors to develop.

**2.** Combine napa cabbage, red cabbage, potatoes and green onions in large bowl; mix well. Add dressing; toss to coat evenly. Sprinkle with sunflower kernels just before serving.

# broccoli italian style

MAKES 4 SERVINGS

1¼ pounds fresh broccoli
2 tablespoons lemon juice
1 teaspoon extra virgin olive oil
1 clove garlic, minced
1 teaspoon chopped fresh Italian parsley
Dash black pepper

**1.** Trim broccoli, discarding tough stems. Cut broccoli into florets with 2-inch stems. Peel remaining stems; cut into ½-inch slices.

**2.** Bring 1 quart water to a boil in large saucepan over medium-high heat. Add broccoli; return to a boil. Cook 3 to 5 minutes or until broccoli is tender. Drain; transfer to serving dish.

**3.** Combine lemon juice, oil, garlic, parsley and pepper in small bowl. Pour over broccoli; toss to coat. Cover and let stand 1 hour before serving to allow flavors to blend. Serve at room temperature.

# millet pilaf

MAKES 6 SERVINGS

1 tablespoon olive oil

½ onion, finely chopped

½ red bell pepper, finely chopped

1 carrot, finely chopped

2 cloves garlic, minced

1 cup uncooked millet

3 cups water

Grated peel and juice of 1 lemon

¾ teaspoon salt

¼ teaspoon black pepper

2 tablespoons chopped fresh parsley (optional)

**1.** Heat oil in medium saucepan over medium heat. Add onion, bell pepper, carrot and garlic; cook and stir 5 minutes or until softened. Add millet; cook and stir 5 minutes or until lightly toasted.

**2.** Stir in water, lemon peel, lemon juice, salt and black pepper; bring to a boil. Reduce heat to low; cover and simmer 30 minutes or until water is absorbed and millet is tender. Cover and let stand 5 minutes. Fluff with fork. Sprinkle with parsley, if desired.

# creamy spinach and brown rice

MAKES 4 SERVINGS

2 teaspoons olive oil

1½ cups sliced mushrooms

½ cup thinly sliced leek, white part only

2 cups fat-free (skim) milk

½ cup uncooked brown rice

⅓ cup shredded low-fat Swiss cheese

1 tablespoon chopped fresh thyme *or* 1 teaspoon dried thyme leaves, crushed

⅛ teaspoon black pepper

2 cups chopped stemmed washed spinach

**1.** Heat oil in medium saucepan over medium-high heat. Add mushrooms and leek; cook and stir until leek is tender.

**2.** Add milk and rice. Bring to a boil over medium-high heat. Reduce heat to medium-low. Cover; simmer 45 to 50 minutes or until rice is tender, stirring frequently. Remove from heat.

**3.** Add cheese, thyme and pepper. Cook and stir until cheese melts. Stir in spinach. Cover; let stand 5 minutes.

# quinoa & mango salad

MAKES 8 SERVINGS

1 cup uncooked quinoa

2 cups water

2 cups cubed peeled mangoes (about 2 large mangoes)

½ cup sliced green onions

½ cup dried cranberries

2 tablespoons chopped fresh parsley

¼ cup extra virgin olive oil

1 tablespoon plus 1½ teaspoons white wine vinegar

1 teaspoon Dijon mustard

½ teaspoon salt

⅛ teaspoon black pepper

**1.** Place quinoa in fine-mesh strainer; rinse well under cold running water. Combine quinoa and 2 cups water in medium saucepan; bring to a boil over high heat. Reduce heat to low; cover and simmer 10 to 12 minutes until quinoa is tender and water is absorbed. Stir quinoa; let stand, covered, 15 minutes. Transfer to large bowl; cover and refrigerate at least 1 hour.

**2.** Add mangoes, green onions, cranberries and parsley to quinoa; mix well.

**3.** Combine oil, vinegar, mustard, salt and pepper in small bowl; whisk until blended. Pour over quinoa mixture; mix until well blended.

**tip:** This salad can be made several hours ahead and refrigerated. Allow it to stand at room temperature for at least 30 minutes before serving.

**note:** Quinoa may seem new to many Americans but it is actually an ancient grain that was grown by Incas. This tiny round whole grain is higher in protein than other grains and contains all eight essential amino acids, so it is considered a complete protein.

# abc slaw

2 green apples, cut into thin strips

1 package (10 ounces) broccoli slaw with carrots

3 stalks celery, cut into thin slices

1 bulb fennel, cut into thin strips

¼ cup creamy salad dressing

1 tablespoon lemon juice

½ teaspoon red pepper flakes

Combine all ingredients in large bowl; mix well. Chill 1 hour before serving.

# desserts &
# SNACKS

## grapefruit sorbet
MAKES 1⅓ CUPS (4 SERVINGS)

1 large pink grapefruit
½ cup apple juice
1 tablespoon sugar

**1.** Peel grapefruit and remove white pith. Cut into segments over bowl to catch juices, removing membranes between segments. Combine grapefruit, grapefruit juice, apple juice and sugar in food processor or blender; purée until smooth.

**2.** Freeze grapefruit mixture in ice cream maker according to manufacturer's directions. Serve immediately.

# taco popcorn olé

MAKES 6 SERVINGS

9 cups air-popped popcorn
½ teaspoon olive oil
1 teaspoon chili powder
½ teaspoon salt
½ teaspoon garlic powder
⅛ teaspoon ground red pepper (optional)

**1.** Preheat oven to 350°F. Line 15×10×1-inch jelly-roll pan with foil.

**2.** Place popcorn in single layer in prepared pan. Drizzle with oil.

**3.** Combine chili powder, salt, garlic powder and ground red pepper, if desired, in small bowl. Sprinkle over popcorn; toss lightly to coat.

**4.** Bake 5 minutes or until heated through, stirring gently after 3 minutes. Spread popcorn in single layer on large sheet of foil to cool.

**tip:** Store popcorn in tightly covered container at room temperature up to 4 days.

# fabulous fruit salad with strawberry vinaigrette

MAKES 6 SERVINGS

2 cups fresh strawberry slices, divided

2 tablespoons canola oil

2 tablespoons lime juice

2 tablespoons red wine vinegar

½ teaspoon sugar

1 bunch watercress, trimmed

1 avocado, sliced

2 cups cantaloupe balls

**1.** Combine 1 cup strawberry slices, oil, lime juice, vinegar and sugar in food processor; process until smooth. Strain mixture through fine-mesh sieve; discard solids.

**2.** Arrange watercress on plates; top with avocado, cantaloupe and remaining 1 cup strawberries. Drizzle with vinaigrette.

# mango-raspberry crisp

## MAKES 4 SERVINGS

1 mango, peeled, seeded and chopped into ½-inch pieces

1 cup fresh raspberries

½ cup old-fashioned oats

1 tablespoon packed brown sugar

½ to 1 teaspoon ground cinnamon

½ teaspoon vegetable oil

2 tablespoons chopped pecans

**1.** Preheat oven to 400°F. Spray 4 custard cups or ramekins with nonstick cooking spray.

**2.** Divide mango and raspberries evenly among custard cups.

**3.** Combine oats, brown sugar and cinnamon in medium bowl. Add oil; mix well. Stir in pecans. Sprinkle evenly over fruit.

**4.** Bake 20 to 25 minutes or until fruit is tender and topping is golden brown. Let stand 15 minutes before serving.

# chocolate gingersnaps

MAKES ABOUT 3 DOZEN COOKIES

½ cup sugar

1 package (15 ounces) gluten-free chocolate cake mix

1 tablespoon ground ginger

2 eggs

⅓ cup vegetable oil

**1.** Preheat oven to 350°F. Line 2 cookie sheets with parchment paper. Place sugar in shallow bowl.

**2.** Combine cake mix and ginger in large bowl. Add eggs and oil; stir until well blended. Shape tablespoonfuls of dough into 1-inch balls; roll in sugar to coat. Place 2 inches apart on prepared cookie sheets.

**3.** Bake 10 minutes or until set. Cool on cookie sheets 2 minutes. Remove to wire racks; cool completely.

# summertime fruit medley

## MAKES 8 SERVINGS

2 large ripe peaches, peeled and sliced

2 large ripe nectarines, sliced

1 large ripe mango, peeled and cut into 1-inch chunks

1 cup fresh blueberries

2 cups orange juice

¼ cup amaretto *or* ½ teaspoon almond extract

1 tablespoon sugar

Fresh mint (optional)

**1.** Combine peaches, nectarines, mango and blueberries in large bowl.

**2.** Whisk orange juice, amaretto and sugar in small bowl until sugar is dissolved. Pour over fruit mixture; toss to coat. Marinate 1 hour at room temperature, gently stirring occasionally. Garnish with fresh mint.

# cranberry fruit salad

MAKES 8 SERVINGS

2  large navel oranges

2  large pink grapefruit

1  cup seedless grapes

2  kiwis, peeled, halved lengthwise and cut into bite-size pieces (½ cup)

¾  cup light cranberry juice cocktail

2  tablespoons dried cranberries (optional)

**1.** Grate orange peel to measure 1 teaspoon. Peel oranges and grapefruit. Cut fruit into segments over large bowl, leaving behind white pith. Squeeze pith and peels over bowl to extract any remaining juice.

**2.** Stir in grapes, kiwi, cranberry juice, cranberries, if desired, and grated orange peel. Serve immediately.

# sippers &
# JUICES

## mango-mint green tea

MAKES 4½ CUPS

3 cups boiling water

6 green tea bags

¼ cup fresh mint leaves

1½ cups mango-peach juice or mango nectar

1 tablespoon sugar

Ice cubes

Fresh mango slices (optional)

Sprigs fresh mint (optional)

**1.** Pour boiling water over tea bags in medium bowl. Let steep for 5 minutes. Remove and discard tea bags.

**2.** Meanwhile, use back of spoon to slightly crush mint leaves.

**3.** Stir mint leaves, mango-peach juice and sugar into tea. Cover and refrigerate 4 to 24 hours.

**4.** Strain tea; discard mint leaves. Serve tea over ice cubes. Garnish with fresh mango slices and mint sprigs.

# apple melon juice

## MAKES 3 SERVINGS

¼ honeydew melon, rind removed

¼ cantaloupe, rind removed

1 apple

3 leaves kale

3 leaves Swiss chard

Juice honeydew, cantaloupe, apple, kale and chard. Stir.

# cabbage patch juice

MAKES 3 SERVINGS

2 apples
¼ napa cabbage
¼ red cabbage

Juice apples, napa cabbage and red cabbage. Stir.

# sparkling tangerine-cranberry green tea

MAKES 4 SERVINGS

2 cups chilled green tea
1 cup freshly squeezed tangerine juice (3 to 4 tangerines)
½ cup cold cranberry juice
1 cup cold seltzer water
Ice cubes
Tangerine slices (optional)
Fresh cranberries (optional)

**1.** Mix tea, tangerine juice, cranberry juice and seltzer in large pitcher.

**2.** Serve immediately in 4 ice-filled glasses. Garnish with tangerine slices and/or cranberries.

# purple pineapple juice

## MAKES 2 SERVINGS

1 beet

1 pear

¼ pineapple, peeled

1 inch fresh ginger, peeled

Juice beet, pear, pineapple and ginger. Stir.

# up and at 'em

## MAKES 1 SERVING

2 cups fresh spinach
1 apple
1 carrot
1 stalk celery
¼ lemon, peeled
1 inch fresh ginger, peeled

Juice spinach, apple, carrot, celery, lemon and ginger. Stir.

# green tea citrus smoothie

4 green tea bags
1 cup boiling water
2 tablespoons sugar
3 tablespoons lemon juice
1 cup frozen lemon sorbet
4 ice cubes, plus additional
for serving
1 cup club soda, chilled
4 lemon wedges

**1.** Place tea bags in heatproof cup or mug. Add boiling water. Steep tea 5 minutes. Remove and discard tea bags. Stir in sugar until dissolved. Refrigerate until cold.

**2.** Combine tea, lemon juice, lemon sorbet and 4 ice cubes in blender. Process about 30 seconds to 1 minute or until mixture is frothy and ice is finely ground. Gently stir in club soda.

**3.** Pour into 4 tall glasses; add additional ice cubes, if desired. Garnish with lemon wedges. Serve immediately.

# blueberry haze

## MAKES 2 SERVINGS

2 apples
1½ cups fresh blueberries
½ grapefruit, peeled
1 inch fresh ginger, peeled

Juice apples, blueberries, grapefruit and ginger. Stir.

# kale melon

MAKES 3 SERVINGS

4 leaves kale

2 apples

⅛ seedless watermelon,
   rind removed

½ lemon, peeled

Juice kale, apples, watermelon and lemon.
Stir.

# mint-green tea coolers

MAKES 2 SERVINGS

2  bags green tea
4  thin slices fresh ginger
    (about 1 inch)
7  or 8 large fresh mint
    leaves, roughly torn
2  cups boiling water
2  cups crushed ice

**1.** Place tea bags, ginger and mint leaves in teapot or 2-cup heatproof measuring cup. Add boiling water; steep 4 minutes. Remove tea bags, ginger and mint leaves; discard. Cool tea to room temperature.

**2.** Pour 1 cup crushed ice into each of 2 tall glasses. Divide tea between glasses.

**tip:** Squeeze a lime wedge (about ⅛ of a lime) into each cooler before serving.

# cantaloupe strawberry sunrise

## MAKES 2 SERVINGS

1 cup cantaloupe chunks
2 clementines, peeled
1 cup frozen strawberries

Combine cantaloupe, clementines and strawberries in blender; blend until smooth. Serve immediately.

# cool apple mango

## MAKES 2 SERVINGS

1 mango, peeled
1 apple
1 cucumber
½ inch fresh ginger, peeled

Juice mango, apple, cucumber and ginger. Stir.

# ruby red delight

MAKES 2 SERVINGS

¼ cup water

1 navel orange, peeled and seeded

1 medium beet, peeled and cut into chunks

½ cup seedless red grapes

½ cup frozen strawberries

¼ teaspoon ground ginger

Combine water, orange, beet, grapes, strawberries and ginger in blender; blend until smooth. Serve immediately.

# immunity booster

## MAKES 3 SERVINGS

1 grapefruit, peeled
2 oranges, peeled
½ cup fresh blackberries

Juice grapefruit, oranges and blackberries. Stir.

# easy being green

MAKES 2 SERVINGS

2 cups watercress
2 parsnips
2 stalks celery
½ cucumber
4 sprigs fresh basil

Juice watercress, parsnips, celery, cucumber and basil. Stir.

# pear avocado smoothie

1½  cups ice
 1  pear, peeled and cubed
 1  cup apple juice
 ½  avocado
 ¼  cup fresh mint leaves
 2  tablespoons fresh lime
     juice

**1.** Place ice, pear, apple juice, avocado, mint and lime juice in blender. Blend until smooth.

**2.** Pour into 2 glasses; serve immediately.

# peaches and green

### MAKES 1 SERVING

¾ cup almond milk
1 cup loosely packed spinach
1 cup frozen sliced peaches
1 cup ice cubes
1 tablespoon honey
⅛ teaspoon vanilla

Combine almond milk, spinach, peaches, ice, honey and vanilla in blender; blend until smooth.

# cherry vanilla chilla

## MAKES 2 SERVINGS

2 ice cubes
¾ cup plain nonfat yogurt
¾ cup frozen cherries
½ cup reduced-fat (2%) milk
1 teaspoon sugar
1½ teaspoons vanilla
2 fresh cherries (optional)

**1.** Crush ice in blender.

**2.** Add remaining ingredients except fresh cherries; blend until smooth.

**3.** Pour into glasses; garnish with fresh cherries.

# island delight smoothie

MAKES 4 SERVINGS

2 cups chopped fresh or jarred mango

1 container (16 ounces) plain nonfat yogurt

1½ cups pineapple-orange juice, chilled

1 cup chopped pineapple

1 frozen banana

½ cup sliced fresh strawberries

1 tablespoon honey

1½ cups ice cubes

Fresh banana slices (optional)

**1.** Combine mango, yogurt, pineapple-orange juice, pineapple, frozen banana, strawberries, honey and ice in blender; process until fruit is puréed and mixture is smooth.

**2.** Pour into 4 glasses. Garnish with banana slices. Serve immediately.

# citrus cooler

MAKES 9 SERVINGS

2 cups fresh orange juice

2 cups unsweetened
pineapple juice

1 teaspoon lemon juice

¾ teaspoon coconut extract

¾ teaspoon vanilla

2 cups cold sparkling water
Ice cubes

**1.** Combine orange juice, pineapple juice, lemon juice, coconut extract and vanilla in large pitcher; refrigerate until cold.

**2.** To serve, stir in sparkling water. Serve in ice-filled glasses.

# index

ABC Slaw ............................ 144

## appetizers

Avocado Salsa ..................... 25

Mini Spinach
Frittatas .......................... 34

Red Pepper Relish ........... 28

Roasted Sweet Potato and
Hoisin Lettuce
Wraps ............................. 30

Apple Melon Juice .............. 162

Apple Stuffed Acorn
Squash .............................. 116

Asian Pesto Noodles ........... 88

Avocado Salsa ......................... 25

## beverages

Apple Melon Juice ......... 162

Blueberry Haze ................. 170

Cabbage Patch
Juice ................................ 163

Cantaloupe Strawberry
Sunrise ............................ 174

Cherry Vanilla
Chilla ............................. 183

Citrus Cooler ..................... 186

Cool Apple Mango ......... 175

Easy Being Green ............. 179

Green Tea Citrus
Smoothie ........................ 168

Immunity Booster ............. 178

Island Delight
Smoothie ....................... 184

Kale Melon ...................... 171

Mango-Mint Green
Tea .................................... 161

Mint-Green Tea
Coolers ............................ 172

Peaches and Green ........ 182

Pear Avocado
Smoothie ....................... 180

Purple Pineapple
Juice ................................ 166

Ruby Red Delight ........... 176

Sparkling Tangerine-
Cranberry Green
Tea .................................... 164

Up and at 'Em .................... 167

Blueberry Haze .................... 170

Breakfast Bites ....................... 26

## breakfasts

Breakfast Bites ................... 26

Scrambled Tofu and
Potatoes ............................ 98

Broccoli Italian Style ......... 136

Broiled Turkey Tenderloin
Kabobs ............................. 72

Brown Rice & Vegetable
Stuffed Squash ............. 96

Buckwheat with Zucchini
and Mushrooms .......... 110

Butternut Squash and Millet
Soup ..................................... 52

Cabbage and Red Potato
Salad with Cilantro-Lime
Dressing .......................... 134

Cabbage Patch Juice ....... 163

Cannellini Bean Stew with
Roasted Tomatoes &
Zucchini ............................ 46

Cantaloupe Strawberry
Sunrise .............................. 174

Cedar Plank Salmon with
Grilled Citrus
Mango ................................ 66

Cherry Vanilla Chilla .......... 183

Chicken and Spinach
Salad ................................. 76

Chicken Soup au
Pistou ................................ 50

Chilled Cucumber
Soup ................................... 48

Chocolate
Gingersnaps ................. 154

Citrus Cooler ........................ 186

Cool Apple Mango .............. 175

Cranberry Fruit
Salad ................................. 158

Creamy Spinach and Brown
Rice ................................. 140

## desserts & sweets

Chocolate Gingersnaps .................. 154

Cranberry Fruit Salad .................. 158

Fabulous Fruit Salad with Strawberry Vinaigrette .................... 150

Grapefruit Sorbet ........... 147

Mango-Raspberry Crisp ........................... 152

Summertime Fruit Medley ............................. 156

Easy Being Green ................. 179

Fabulous Fruit Salad with Strawberry Vinaigrette ..................... 150

## fish & seafood

Asian Pesto Noodles ............................... 88

Cedar Plank Salmon with Grilled Citrus Mango .................................. 66

Gazpacho Shrimp Salad ................................. 59

Grilled Tilapia with Zesty Mustard Sauce ............... 70

Pan-Seared Sole with Lemon-Butter Caper Sauce .................................. 74

Roast Dill Scrod with Asparagus ......................... 78

Roast Sesame Fish ............ 86

Roasted Salmon with New Potatoes and Red Onions ............................... 60

Salmon Salad with Basil Vinaigrette ......................... 84

Fukien Red-Cooked Pork ................................. 68

Gazpacho Shrimp Salad .................................. 59

Grapefruit Sorbet ............... 147

Greek Chicken & Spinach Rice Casserole ............... 62

Green Tea Citrus Smoothie ......................... 168

Grilled Tilapia with Zesty Mustard Sauce .............. 70

Hot and Sour Soup with Bok Choy and Tofu .............. 42

Immunity Booster ............... 178

Island Delight Smoothie ......................... 184

Italian Escarole and White Bean Stew ......................... 54

Italian Skillet Roasted Vegetable Soup ........... 40

Kale & Mushroom Stuffed Chicken Breasts ........... 82

Kale Melon ................................. 171

Light Lemon Cauliflower ...................... 126

Mandarin Chicken Salad .................................. 64

Mango-Mint Green Tea ........................................ 161

Mango-Raspberry Crisp ............................. 152

Marinated Vegetables ..... 130

## meatless meals

Brown Rice & Vegetable Stuffed Squash .............. 96

Buckwheat with Zucchini and Mushrooms .......... 110

Quinoa with Tomato, Broccoli and Feta ......... 93

Quinoa-Stuffed Eggplant ........................ 100

Roasted Vegetable Salad with Capers and Walnuts ............................ 108

Soba Stir-Fry ...................... 94

Spicy Sesame Noodles ............................ 102

Vegetarian Paella .............. 112

Vegetarian Quinoa Chili .................................. 104

Zucchini and Sweet Potato Stuffed Peppers ......... 106

Mediterranean Vegetable Bake ............................... 124

Millet Pilaf ................................. 138

Mini Spinach Frittatas ........ 34

Mini Turkey Loaves ............. 32

Mint-Green Tea Coolers ............................ 172

Miso Soup with Tofu ........... 39

Monterey Potato Hash .................................. 36

Nutty Vegetable Duo ......... 115

Pan-Seared Sole with
   Lemon-Butter Caper
   Sauce ................................. 74

Peaches and Green ............ 182

Pear Avocado
   Smoothie ........................ 180

## pork

Fukien Red-Cooked
   Pork .................................. 68

Pork Tenderloin with
   Cabbage ........................... 80

Pork Tenderloin with
   Cabbage ........................... 80

## poultry

Broiled Turkey Tenderloin
   Kabobs ............................. 72

Chicken and Spinach
   Salad ............................... 76

Greek Chicken & Spinach
   Rice Casserole ............... 62

Kale & Mushroom Stuffed
   Chicken Breasts ........... 82

Mandarin Chicken
   Salad ............................... 64

Mini Turkey Loaves .......... 32

Sizzling Rice Flour
   Crêpes ............................ 90

Purple Pineapple
   Juice ............................... 166

Quinoa & Mango
   Salad ............................... 142

Quinoa with Tomato,
   Broccoli and Feta ......... 93

Quinoa-Stuffed
   Eggplant ....................... 100

Red Pepper Relish ............... 28

Roast Dill Scrod with
   Asparagus ....................... 78

Roast Sesame Fish ............... 86

Roasted Salmon with New
   Potatoes and Red
   Onions ............................. 60

Roasted Sweet Potato and
   Apple Salad .................... 122

Roasted Sweet Potato and
   Hoisin Lettuce
   Wraps ................................ 30

Roasted Vegetable Salad
   with Capers and
   Walnuts .......................... 108

Ruby Red Delight ............... 176

## salads

ABC Slaw .......................... 144

Cabbage and Red Potato
   Salad with Cilantro-Lime
   Dressing .......................... 134

Quinoa & Mango
   Salad ............................... 142

Roasted Sweet Potato and
   Apple Salad .................... 122

Spicy Grapefruit Salad
   with Raspberry
   Dressing ........................... 132

Spinach Salad with
   Pomegranate
   Vinaigrette ..................... 128

Sweet & Savory Sweet
   Potato Salad ................. 120

Salmon Salad with Basil
   Vinaigrette ...................... 84

Scrambled Tofu and
   Potatoes ........................... 98

## side dishes

Apple Stuffed Acorn
   Squash ............................. 116

Broccoli Italian Style .... 136

Creamy Spinach and
   Brown Rice ................... 140

Light Lemon
   Cauliflower ..................... 126

Marinated
   Vegetables ..................... 130

Mediterranean Vegetable
   Bake ................................ 124

Millet Pilaf ........................... 138

Monterey Potato
   Hash ................................. 36

Nutty Vegetable Duo .... 115

Veggie-Quinoa and Brown
   Rice Pilaf ......................... 118

Sizzling Rice Flour
   Crêpes ............................ 90

Slow Cooker Veggie
   Stew ......................... 44

**snacks**

Taco Popcorn Olé ........... 148

Soba Stir-Fry ........................ 94

**soups & stews**

Butternut Squash and
   Millet Soup ..................... 52
Cannellini Bean Stew with
   Roasted Tomatoes &
   Zucchini ........................ 46
Chicken Soup au
   Pistou ............................ 50
Chilled Cucumber
   Soup ............................... 48

Hot and Sour Soup with
   Bok Choy and
   Tofu ........................... 42
Italian Escarole and White
   Bean Stew ..................... 54
Italian Skillet Roasted
   Vegetable Soup .......... 40
Miso Soup with Tofu ........ 39
Slow Cooker Veggie
   Stew ............................. 44
Vegetarian Chili ............... 56

Sparkling Tangerine-
   Cranberry Green
   Tea ............................... 164
Spicy Grapefruit Salad with
   Raspberry
   Dressing ........................ 132

Spicy Sesame
   Noodles ....................... 102
Spinach Salad with
   Pomegranate
   Vinaigrette .................... 128
Summertime Fruit
   Medley .......................... 156
Sweet & Savory Sweet
   Potato Salad ................. 120
Taco Popcorn Olé ............. 148
Up and at 'Em ................... 167
Vegetarian Chili ................. 56
Vegetarian Paella ................ 112
Vegetarian Quinoa
   Chili ............................... 104
Veggie-Quinoa and Brown
   Rice Pilaf ........................ 118
Zucchini and Sweet Potato
   Stuffed Peppers ......... 106

# metric conversion chart

## VOLUME MEASUREMENTS (dry)

$^1/_8$ teaspoon = 0.5 mL
$^1/_4$ teaspoon = 1 mL
$^1/_2$ teaspoon = 2 mL
$^3/_4$ teaspoon = 4 mL
1 teaspoon = 5 mL
1 tablespoon = 15 mL
2 tablespoons = 30 mL
$^1/_4$ cup = 60 mL
$^1/_3$ cup = 75 mL
$^1/_2$ cup = 125 mL
$^2/_3$ cup = 150 mL
$^3/_4$ cup = 175 mL
1 cup = 250 mL
2 cups = 1 pint = 500 mL
3 cups = 750 mL
4 cups = 1 quart = 1 L

## VOLUME MEASUREMENTS (fluid)

1 fluid ounce (2 tablespoons) = 30 mL
4 fluid ounces ($^1/_2$ cup) = 125 mL
8 fluid ounces (1 cup) = 250 mL
12 fluid ounces (1$^1/_2$ cups) = 375 mL
16 fluid ounces (2 cups) = 500 mL

## WEIGHTS (mass)

$^1/_2$ ounce = 15 g
1 ounce = 30 g
3 ounces = 90 g
4 ounces = 120 g
8 ounces = 225 g
10 ounces = 285 g
12 ounces = 360 g
16 ounces = 1 pound = 450 g

## DIMENSIONS

$^1/_{16}$ inch = 2 mm
$^1/_8$ inch = 3 mm
$^1/_4$ inch = 6 mm
$^1/_2$ inch = 1.5 cm
$^3/_4$ inch = 2 cm
1 inch = 2.5 cm

## OVEN TEMPERATURES

250°F = 120°C
275°F = 140°C
300°F = 150°C
325°F = 160°C
350°F = 180°C
375°F = 190°C
400°F = 200°C
425°F = 220°C
450°F = 230°C

## BAKING PAN SIZES

| Utensil | Size in Inches/Quarts | Metric Volume | Size in Centimeters |
|---|---|---|---|
| Baking or Cake Pan (square or rectangular) | 8×8×2 | 2 L | 20×20×5 |
| | 9×9×2 | 2.5 L | 23×23×5 |
| | 12×8×2 | 3 L | 30×20×5 |
| | 13×9×2 | 3.5 L | 33×23×5 |
| Loaf Pan | 8×4×3 | 1.5 L | 20×10×7 |
| | 9×5×3 | 2 L | 23×13×7 |
| Round Layer Cake Pan | 8×1½ | 1.2 L | 20×4 |
| | 9×1½ | 1.5 L | 23×4 |
| Pie Plate | 8×1¼ | 750 mL | 20×3 |
| | 9×1¼ | 1 L | 23×3 |
| Baking Dish or Casserole | 1 quart | 1 L | — |
| | 1½ quart | 1.5 L | — |
| | 2 quart | 2 L | — |